Yak Butter & Black Tea

Yak Butter
& Black Tea

A Journey into Tibet

WADE BRACKENBURY

Algonquin Books

of Chapel Hill

1998

Published by
Algonquin Books of Chapel Hill
Post Office Box 2225
Chapel Hill, North Carolina 27515-2225

a division of
Workman Publishing
708 Broadway
New York, New York 10003

Published simultaneously in Canada by
    Thomas Allen & Son Limited.
First paperback edition, March 1998. Originally published
    in hardcover by Algonquin Books of Chapel Hill in 1997.
Design by Bonnie Campbell.

Library of Congress Cataloging-in-Publication Data
Brackenbury, Wade, 1964–
    Yak butter and black tea : a journey into forbidden China /
Wade Brackenbury.
        p.   cm.
    ISBN 1-56512-148-1
    1. Brackenbury, Wade, 1964–   —Journeys—China.
2. Tibet (China)—Description and travel.   3. Yunnan Province
(China)—Description and travel.   4. Tulung (Tibeto-Burman
people)—China—Yunnan Province.   I. Title.
    DS712.B68   1997
    915.1'50459—dc20   96-30756
                                                    CIP

ISBN 1-56512-201-1 paper

10 9 8 7 6 5 4 3 2

For my father, Phil Brackenbury

Acknowledgments

MY GRATITUDE FIRST and foremost to my mother (and high school English teacher) Margaret Brackenbury, who has always shown great support and encouragement for all of my endeavors, and who also typed this entire manuscript—many times.

Thanks to Pascal Szapu and Sophi Tcheng, with whom I shared the adventures herein.

Thanks also to Robert Rubin, senior editor at Algonquin, whose enthusiasm and approachability allayed many of my fears, making publishing my first book a fun experience. I also want to express my gratitude to Amy Gash and Bonnie Levy for their editing.

For invaluable help in editing my initial journals into book form, thanks to Dr. Don Norton, professor of English at Brigham Young University, and a great inspiration to me in many ways. Thanks also to Louanna Clark for her tireless line editing, to Janet Canniff for clarification and accurate description of Catholic ordinances, and to Khangdo Chazotsang, niece to His Holiness the fourteenth Dalai Lama, and her husband, Rapten, for their friendship and help in understanding Tibetan culture.

Even before there was any serious talk of writing a book, many people read my journals and gave invaluable feedback, which I was later to incorporate into my writing.

Among those are Bonnie and Bill Sweet, Mike Wilkinson, Carol Beeton, Kathy Steenstra, Dale Speiser, Amy and Mike Danielson, Iva Brackenbury, Tim and Amy Kaser, Ilene Thompson, Laura Olsen, Dave and Martha Christenson, Holly Zardus and her family, Lana Parker, Lennie Eisenhauer, George Dille, and Carolyn Buttorf. Thanks to Matt Williamson for computer expertise — at all hours of the day or night — and to Judy Stroud for encouragement through the years.

I want to express my gratitude to Dennis Thompson, Eric Thomas, Carolyn Sly, and the late Professor David Thompson for teaching and sharing with me their wilderness knowledge and skills. And I want to thank L. Jay Michelle for his equally valuable insights into the inner wilderness of human nature.

Thanks to Liza Paschal and the folks at the Elephant's Perch in Sun Valley, Idaho, for help in selecting gear for this and many other trips. Thanks to Jo An Schranz, who dropped everything to custom-make equipment for my trips. To my business manager, Leslie Bennett, for keeping things rolling when my mind swept back to Tibet for days at a time during rewrites. And to Dr. Gerald Clum, president of Life College of Chiropractic West, for making it possible for me to take time off from school.

A special thanks to authors David Quammen, Lee Nelson, and Frith Maier for unselfishly sharing with me their hard-learned knowlege of the publishing world. And a very special thanks to Daniel Hays for introducing me to Robert and the folks at Algonquin and for showing me through example the importance of living the dream.

Contents

A Legend

A LONG TIME ago when the world was young, the land was covered with people. The forests were filled with the sounds of many kinds of animals, all good for food. The good soil produced more corn and vegetables and barley than all the people could eat, so there was plenty of everything for all and no reason for unhappiness. These people were all the same and spoke the same language, but the gods of the heavens became displeased because these people did not recognize their good fortune or show proper gratitude. So one day the gods allowed a great flood to come upon the land. It came so quickly no one had time to find their boats or to run away to the high mountains, but one little boy and his sister were high in the mountains collecting berries. When the floods came, they ran even higher and so saved themselves from drowning. When the water went away, they retreated to the valley below only to find that no one else had survived the flood. They were very sad and lonely. Shortly afterward the gods came down from heaven and commanded them to marry and have children to fill the earth as it had been before, but because they were sister and brother, they refused and would not marry. Many times the gods came and told them they had to do this, but just as many times they said it was impossible. One day the boy, now a young man, was swimming alone

in a quiet pool on the Lancang River. The gods caused a
great thirst to come upon the girl and she immediately went
to the river edge and drank deeply from the water. Soon
after her belly and breasts began to swell and she knew that
she was carrying her brother's child. So it was with water
that the people were destroyed and again water that started
the propagation of a new civilization. When the hour for
delivery finally arrived, a great bottle came out of the girl's
womb. This bottle was of smooth clay and had nine tiers,
like the floors of a pagoda. The girl and boy were frightened, and the bottle slipped from their shaking hands.
When it struck the earth, it broke into nine pieces, which
rolled in different directions across the earth. Each of these
pieces became a separate people with a separate language.
The tier that rolled the farthest west became the Drung and
the Nu people.

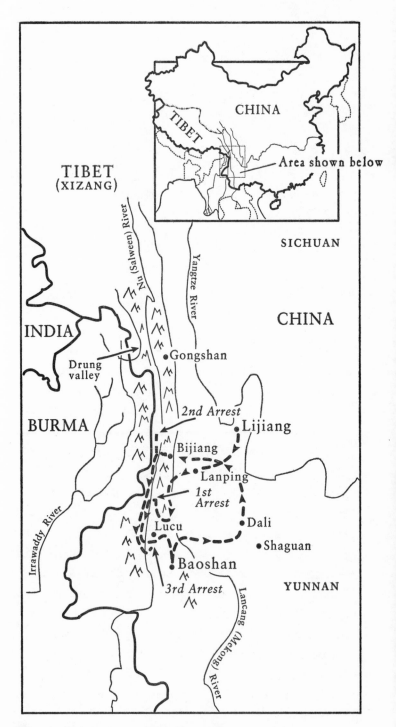

First Journey with Pascal

The Forbidden Valley

I HAD ORIGINALLY come to China's Yunnan Province to climb. A snapshot of the pristine Jade Dragon mountain had lured me out of college and across the ocean to China, where I had hopes of soloing on at least one of its lower peaks.

Growing up in the tiny, conservative town of Fairfield, in central Idaho, I had never imagined that at age twenty-nine I would still be single or a student. But in my junior year of high school a freak football injury had changed the course of my entire life. Partially crippled and in constant pain, I spent the next three years in a living hell, a hodge-podge of doctors, hospitals, and high school home study. Nevertheless, at age nineteen I had entirely recovered (at least physically), had my high school diploma, and was eagerly preparing to start college, find a girlfriend, and begin paving my way toward a bright, prosperous future. But after the first semester, and to the great surprise of everyone, I decided to take a year off to go climbing in New Zealand—just one big adventure before settling down for good, I thought and said. But just three years later I found myself again taking off, this time to ride a dirt bike across Mexico. Next it was a voyage down the Rio Pasión of Guatemala on a small raft I'd built near the headwaters.

Between these trips I'd plug away at school for a year

or two, reasonably happy and dedicated and getting good grades. I'm certain no one who knew me had any inkling of the deep, gnawing discontent that would grow with each passing day until *wham!* something I heard or read would bring these feelings raging to the surface as turbulent, poignant longings for faraway places, exotic cultures, high adventures, and mystical experiences. Next would follow a short, all-consuming preparation, and then, once again, I would be off to someplace like the Great Barrier Reef of Australia or the highlands of Papua New Guinea.

Eventually, my travels had brought me here to Asia, where I had spent the better part of three years. This was my first trip to southern China, though. I knew about this area only through the books I'd read. I knew, for instance, that for the last twenty years the Chinese government had been repeatedly and harshly criticized by the international community for its supression of minority cultures within its borders, the most famous of which was their oppression of Tibet. In recent years, this problem had been compounded by the emergence of renewed Chinese nationalism, which many of the non-Chinese minorities wanted nothing to do with. Since minorities were such a politically sensitive subject in China, much of Yunnan Province, near the borders of Burma and India, was strictly closed to foreigners. Of the fifty-five officially recognized Chinese minorities (which make up less then 5 percent of the total population), twenty-five lived here in Yunnan.

But I wasn't really interested in politics. I had come to Yunnan looking for adventure.

HAVING ARRIVED ONLY hours earlier in the city of Lijiang with my friend and traveling companion Holly Zardis from

Jackson Hole, Wyoming, I had just sat down to a big meal of fried bread and meat in a little Naxi ethnic restaurant when we noticed a tall, rawboned man with sandy hair and gold wire-rim spectacles resting his elbows on the table beside us. A powerful set of shoulders and arms bulged out, filling the sleeves of his green Chinese bush jacket, the front pocket of which showed the outline of a pack of cigarettes. He hunched forward, apparently oblivious to us, as he pored intently over a faded orange map of South Tibet. Curiosity finally got the better of us, and we asked him what he was so intent on. He snapped his head up as if startled, then smiled warmly and invited us to join him at his table.

In the conversation that followed we learned that he was a freelance photojournalist, and that he made his living taking pictures—sometimes with proper authorization, but most often illegally—of places in Asia that were normally off-limits to foreigners. He spoke confidently and with the fire of someone possessed of great purpose. This, and his heavy French accent, reminded me of a childhood hero, Jacques Cousteau.

What a fascinating job, I thought. Like something out of an Indiana Jones movie!

His name was Pascal Szapu, and he went on to tell us of a remote valley in the Irrawaddy River basin in South Tibet, near the border of Burma, where lived a minority people called the Drung, a people that he believed had yet to be visited and photographed by Westerners. And he was determined to go there.

The Drung valley, he said, nestled between two rugged mountain ranges, whose passes accumulated massive snowpacks in the winter, closing the roads until late summer. It effectively isolated the people there from the rest of China for six to eight months of the year. With a loose head count of between four and five thousand, the Drung people were possibly the smallest minority left in China.

Why, Pascal wanted to know, was this area so tightly closed to foreigners? How much, if any, interaction did the Chinese have with the Drung? And were the Drung, as well as the neighboring Nu and Lisu minorities, subject to oppression by the Chinese authorities?

His two previous attempts to go there had failed, he said. He had first been turned back by huge snowdrifts in the Nu Mountains and later arrested by the Chinese police while attempting a different route. Now he was looking for someone, preferably with some mountaineering experience, to make a third attempt. He said he would be willing to pay expenses, if necessary, and he needed a minimum of one month's commitment.

Within an hour of our first meeting I had said good-bye to Holly and changed all of my travel plans to accommodate four to six extra weeks with Pascal. It sounded like the adventure of a lifetime. I had no idea what I was getting into.

THE VERY NEXT day I found myself wedged between the large Frenchman and a rattling window in the back of a rickety Chinese bus. The ticket lady threw a fit when we showed up to board that morning, because the bus was heading deep into an area of Yunnan strictly forbidden to foreigners. We shoved our way on anyway. I was certain that we would be greeted by the police in the first large city, but just before arriving, Pascal stood up and began slamming the flat of his hand loudly against the roof of the bus.

"Xinar?" ("Where are we?") he demanded, indicating that we were on the wrong bus.

The perplexed driver stopped and let us off. We pretended to start walking back in the direction we had come until the bus drove out of view. Then we turned and hiked into the mountains. Disguising ourselves in Chinese clothing, we spent the next three weeks hiding in the back of ore trucks, sneaking through cities and villages at night, and playing cat and mouse with the authorities. At times we left the roads behind and entered the thick rain forests that blanket the mountains of southeast Yunnan. We crossed mountains and rivers and photographed the inhabitants of remote villages. Once we emerged blinking from the wilderness to find ourselves looking at Bijiang, an eerie, mostly deserted city perched high above the Nu (or Salween) River. The former inhabitants were apparently buried on the hill above, and unruly villagers scurried about like mice in the once-elegant buildings.

We continued north on our quest for the Forbidden Valley, the Valley of the Drung, but we never got there. The monsoons came early. We were rained on and snowed on. My heavy boots rotted, then fell apart. Though Pascal had no reservations about blatantly breaking the law in a communist country, it soon became apparent that he was afraid of the wilderness. To avoid the mountains and wild areas, he began to make sudden changes in our travel route, changes that put us at greater risk of being caught by the authorities. We were arrested twice, once at gunpoint. Both times Pascal turned the tables, insisting we were merely lost tourists who were being badly mistreated. Both times his act so convinced the police of our innocence that they apologized, paid for our hotel room, and provided free transportation out of the closed areas.

Pascal's scams were amazingly clever, and I found myself drawn in, increasingly delighted to participate in them. But they seemed slightly immoral at the same time, and I worried too about getting into real trouble should our shenanigans be brought to light.

My worst fears were realized soon after our second arrest. The Fugong Police District graciously agreed to transport us down the Nu River by jeep. However, in the town of Lucu, near where we had been stopped the first time, we were recognized. The police there were furious at being tricked. We were strip-searched and held for questioning. The next day, a Lisu man from a remote village hiked into town to report that a little girl had become ill following our stay there. He blamed it on some candy I had given her. Charges were brought against me and I was interrogated all night long. I was terrified.

Within three days, Pascal had caused such a commotion with the authorities that he managed to get us released and kicked out of the area, back to an "open" part of China. Soon we were back in Dali, a quaint little tourist city well away from the closed areas. Pascal was already talking with great enthusiasm about the next attempt.

Even though we'd never gotten near the Drung valley, it had been a thrilling few weeks, but I'd had enough. I realized that Pascal could talk nearly anyone into anything, so before he could convince me otherwise, I arose early the next morning and left my good-bye in a note. I traveled alone to Manchuria to climb in the Chunbia Mountains, then flew home to America.

I looked back on that trip with Pascal as a sort of delirious dream—a great story to tell, a memory to treasure as I established a stable life and a solid career for myself. I enrolled in chiropractic school. Someday, I told myself, I would return to China. I never thought I'd see Pascal again.

Yak Butter & Black Tea

PART I

Westward

Second Journey with Pascal and Sophi

ONE

Back to Asia

IT WAS AUGUST of 1993 and I was flying to Hong Kong. Mainland China spread out below my plane in a pastel-colored blanket of red mountains and green valleys. We passed over the city of Shanghai, which looked like the center of a great spider web with its many connecting roads. Shortly before we reached Hong Kong the clouds thickened beneath us and the plane began to bounce and shake violently. The flight attendant came on the intercom and announced in a shaking voice that we were on the fringe of a tropical storm, a typhoon, and that the landing was going to be rough. As the plane pitched and yawed I gripped the armrests tightly and found that my face was suddenly sweaty. Most of the Chinese people around me shrieked loudly, although amazingly enough, some of them were laughing. Just as we came through the clouds a downdraft slammed us toward the runway. Somehow the timing was perfect and there wasn't even a bump. We were on the ground and the nightmare was over.

Pascal met me at the gate. We lugged my bags to a small guest house at Chungking Mansion, in downtown Kowloon, and, after dumping them in our room, went out to an English pub for dinner.

"I still think we can be about certain no one has been

there yet," Pascal again told me as he drank beer with one hand and gesticulated wildly with the other. "I have continued to search the archives in the best museums in France, yet still the only references I can find are over one hundred years old, and they are mostly for the lower, tropical Drung area." His voice rose with each sentence, and his precisely articulated English deteriorated into a rough patois. Two British women sitting in the booth next to us had stopped eating and were staring nervously at him. He looked around sheepishly, calmed himself down, and started speaking in passionate whispers again. "I don't know, Wade. I don't know if we can be successful this time, but if we can, for me it should be the greatest! I want so much to be the first to go there and to take pictures."

Since our last unsuccessful trip into the closed area of Yunnan—or the Forbidden Zone, as Pascal liked to call it—Pascal had been sending me envelopes bulging with maps, drawings, and route proposals to the Drung valley. With each new letter I lost an entire night's sleep. I had finally committed—much to the relief of my parents—to becoming a chiropractor. School was proving to be intense but fascinating, and I had a good relationship with a steady girlfriend. It seemed crazy to interrupt all that now and head off to Asia on another wild adventure.

And yet, here I was in Hong Kong at Pascal's invitation, not only planning to do it again but infused with the same excitement I had felt when we first met in that little Naxi restaurant more than two years before.

Back in the hotel we began the tedious task of sorting through the materials we had prepared for the trip. We knew from our first trip that entire cities and many roads were simply not marked on any map. We had aerial flight charts of a 1:500,000 scale, the only topographic maps readily obtainable for these areas of Tibet, Burma, and China. Pascal had also obtained many other non-topo maps, some of which detailed roads, bridges, towns, or monasteries that weren't found on the others. He had then computer-generated a single map containing all the information from each. Using a grid system of numbers and letters, he'd fed into the computer all the information he was able to find about different areas we might pass through, and had produced a written key. If we could figure out exactly where we were on the map, we would know a little about what to expect in regard to the people and terrain. I marveled at Pascal's dedication, for to produce this must have taken a tremendous amount of time and effort. And this time we had another advantage: a translator.

I had yet to meet Sophi, but there were things about her that worried Pascal. "You must remember, Wade, that to the Chinese, Sophi is Chinese! She is not half French, she is not special. If we get into trouble again, we must take care of her. I am afraid she might not receive the same treatment we will. As for Sophi doing well, she's strong physically and very determined. As far as I can tell, she is the best we can hope for. But we won't know how she is, of course, as you said, until we are in a difficult situation. So we must expect that all will go well with her. And if it doesn't, then of course we can have the necessary confrontation."

I, too, had some deep reservations about bringing her along. In Pascal's more recent letters, he had begun making eloquent reference to Sophi's good looks, at least as often as he had originally praised her language skills. I began to wonder if French libido was starting to push aside common sense.

The next morning Pascal went to the airport to pick up Sophi while I took our passports to a travel agency to apply for visas. A short British man with a little pot belly, a goatee, and two earrings listened imperturbably when I blew up at his proposal to charge each of us 125 Hong Kong dollars extra for four-month visas. I stormed out of the office. "You can always try walking the bloody things through yourself!" he blandly called after me. I tried to calm down, reminding myself that I was back in Asia, where if you didn't know the location of the back door, more than likely you would end up paying someone who did.

I stomped up the stairs and slammed open the door to our room. "Pascal! You won't believe—" When I saw Sophi, I stopped. She was beautiful—slight-built yet full-figured, with olive skin, probably not much over a hundred pounds. She was dressed conservatively in dark cotton pants and a powder-blue button-down shirt. Her hair was butched clear off, though slightly longer in the front, which gave her a distinctly European look.

"Wade, this is Sophi." I self-consciously kissed her on both cheeks. She smiled, seeming to ignore my awkwardness, and stepped back, her eyes sparkling. Pascal spread his hands wide in an all-encompassing gesture. "We will be a great team together." We all laughed.

WE SPENT THE next few days shopping. Pascal and Sophi had both brought a bare minimum of clothes, and after some discussion, Pascal persuaded me to also trim down, although I insisted on retaining a few more articles of warm gear than they did. I hate being cold. Among our purchases: a rope and other miscellaneous climbing gear, an altimeter, and most important for Pascal, 110 rolls of fresh film from a professional outlet. Pascal had brought along ten watertight watches, a collection of color photographs of the Dalai Lama, and other small trinkets we could use for trade and as gifts in Tibet.

One evening I finally had time to look up Doug and Seutsan Cruzan, college friends who had graduated a few months before and opened a chiropractic office in Hong Kong.

"Now, where exactly is this Drung valley, and why are you going there?" Doug asked. An average-size American with curly black hair, he had an infectious enthusiasm for whatever he was discussing.

"It's on the Irrawaddy River, on the border of Burma, India, and Tibet," I answered, hearing my own voice rise with excitement. "Pascal has researched the Drung for over five years, and there is no indication that anyone from the West has been there. If we make it, we'll be first!"

Doug looked at me and laughed. "Just come back alive," he said.

"And what does Jane think of this?" Seutsan asked, referring to my Chinese girlfriend of the past two years. I admitted I had broken up with her while preparing for this trip.

We walked around the city on Hong Kong Island until late, Doug and Seutsan holding hands and laughing. They seemed happier than I could ever remember, which made me think soberly about my decision to come on this expedition and consequently set my own graduation date back by six more months. But it's worth it, I told myself. Worth it to be the first. The subway closed at midnight, so at the last minute I said good-bye to my two friends and jumped on the train back to Kowloon.

In the seat ahead of me a couple in their early twenties snuggled close and held hands. His lips brushed her shiny coal-black hair, and I caught the glimpse of a diamond engagement ring. Then there was a loud hiss of air as the pneumatic door slid open, and I wandered out into the streets of Kowloon alone. Loud music, both Chinese and Western, faded in and out as I wound through narrow brick back alleys past the windowless doors of nightclubs. Familiar melodies tugged at hidden strings—as had Doug and Seutsan's innocent questions. What *was* I doing here? Eventually I came to a small asphalt trail that led into the hills where I had run on previous trips to Hong Kong. A sick burst of adrenaline surged through me as a jackrabbit bounded into the path, saw me, and froze, then before my eyes metamorphosed into a scraggly gray alley cat and padded down into the bushes. Why a jackrabbit? I wondered. What had made me think I saw a prairie jackrabbit here in China? Spontaneously I started jogging, then exploded into a full-out sprint. The city lights reflected pale silver on the cement retaining walls. As I crested the first knoll, my muscles burned and my heart pounded, but I continued to push until the pain and euphoria of exertion drowned out the other feelings.

TWO

Into Tibet

BY AUGUST 25 it was time to fly to Chengdu, the capital of Sichuan Province, which borders Tibet. Our five days in Hong Kong had been busy but wonderful. Pascal knew every good restaurant, every French buffet, and the happy hour of each pub. As a practicing Mormon, I don't drink—which put me in some awkward positions later—but here, where language was no barrier, happy hours were fun and relaxing. Now it was time to move on and start the second phase of the journey. We arrived late in the evening in Chengdu International Airport. From there it was an hour bus ride into the city. Sophi took over, and I realized how great it was to know for sure we were on the right bus and to be able to tell the driver exactly where to drop us off.

The Traffic Hotel—the main guest house for backpackers—was full, so we had to stay in an awful place built underground in some old tunnels that must once have been bomb shelters. The doors were solid concrete, about a foot thick, and swung slowly shut on massive cast-iron hinges. I was separated from Pascal and Sophi and ended up in a tiny cell-like room with a Chinese girl and her boyfriend from the States. She was claustrophobic and had to sleep with the light on. Each time she had to go to the bathroom, she would awaken her boyfriend (and me too) so he could walk her there. In the morning she said her neck and back were killing her, so I performed a chiropractic adjustment on her before checking out. Pascal swore he would sleep in the street before staying another night in that hellhole, but luckily we got a room in the Traffic Hotel, where we stayed two more days while making final preparations before leaving for Tibet.

The most important item of business was to obtain Chinese money. Foreigners are issued FEC (foreign exchange currency) at the bank and are expected to make their purchases using only that. However, the currency can be sold on the black market at a rate of about 1 to 1.4 because the Chinese want FEC to buy things that are not normally available to them from "friendship stores." In 1982, when China opened its doors to foreigners, they set up these stores for foreigners living and traveling in China so that they could buy goods and products not rationed to the general population. It's illegal for ordinary Chinese citizens to possess this currency, but it's impossible to obtain certain goods, such as imported television sets, cameras, and tape players, without it.

At first we had a terrible time finding anyone to change our FECs, which was strange because usually the cities were crawling with greasy young thugs who made their living in this risky way. It was also distressing, because we had to have *renminbi*, as Chinese currency is called, for our trip. It was not just a matter of getting a good deal. FECs would simply not be usable in remote or closed areas. We later learned there had been a big police bust on the black market just days before we had arrived.

The first day, we walked the streets for hours but found only one man who would change our money, and he would change just a little and at a very bad rate. Over the next few days we were able to change the rest, ten thousand yuan (about two thousand U.S. dollars). Even in hundred-yuan notes, which were much too big for our use in Tibet, it was a huge volume of paper. We divided it among the three of us, and the next step was to try to turn it into much smaller amounts by breaking each note on some little purchase, a tedious and aggravating process. Vendors grimaced, then stiffly handed back our money, unwilling to give out change for such large bills. We purchased other needed articles for our trip—tin drinking cups, more medicine, and grain bags to cover and camouflage our backpacks—but still had most of our money in hundred-yuan notes.

WE HEADED WEST by bus toward the Yangtze River. After two days of continuous jarring but spectacular scenery, we arrived in Kangding, which is nominally part of Sichuan but marks the beginning of the part of China inhabited by Tibetans. We passed close to Gongga Shan (known to climbers as Minya Konka), thought at one time to be the highest mountain in the world, but heavy rain prevented us from seeing it. The road wound tortuously along the steep canyon walls of solid and not-so-solid limestone. Our bus sputtered and heaved when we crawled over passes in first gear, then *whee!*—down the other side we rushed as the driver made up for lost time. In order to conserve fuel, the drivers in this part of China typically turned off their engines and coasted down the hills in neutral, relying entirely on their brakes for control. All trucks had a large tank behind the cab that was kept full of water. The water continually flowed down tiny hoses onto the brake drums, which would otherwise burn out in minutes on one of the treacherous descents. If the brakes failed, the trucks could plunge thousands of feet into a gorge. It reminded me of our first trip, when we had witnessed a rock slide. We were riding a bus to Lanping when we rounded a corner and saw rocks spilling across the road. The driver slowed for an instant, and then, to our horror, gunned the engine and tried to bounce us through before the road became totally blocked. *Thud! Crash!* Several boulders slammed into the side of the bus, causing us to skid wildly to one side. A moment later we were through. As the driver jammed on the brakes, I heard a moan and looked back. The seat behind us was covered with glass, blood, and hair. A large chunk of rock had come through the window and now lay in the aisle. An old man had blocked most of the flying glass with his body and been struck on the head by the rock. A jagged laceration ran nearly the length of his scalp. A young boy had also been struck in the face by flying glass and had several deep cuts. A second sooner and the rock would have hit Pascal and me; two seconds sooner and it would have hit the driver. Pascal and I patched up the injured passengers the best we could, using our first-aid kit.

When we reached the next town, nearly an hour later, I helped the old country doctor stitch up the man's head. The little office was unbelievably small and filthy, its dirt floor covered with duck and chicken manure. As we worked, ducks waddled around near the door, occasionally poking their heads in to see if some edible morsel from the surgery had been dropped on the floor. Though I hadn't washed my hands, the doctor had me hold the flap of skin in place. His large, curved stitching needle was still stained with blood from the last patient; he wiped it off with a little alcohol before starting. I had bandaged up the boy's face after the accident. The doctor stared in bewilderment at the plastic butterfly strips, then left them in place. He injected the old man with twenty milligrams of morphine and gave him prescriptions of amoxicillin and oral codeine, after which, with a dreamy look in his eyes, his patient ate a little rice, donned a new hat the bus driver had bought him to cover his wound, and off we went again.

Now I practiced my Mandarin, which I'd studied sporadically for the last two years, but mostly we had to rely on Sophi's translations. We joked back and forth with the Chinese people, and after much insistence, I even sang an American pop song, at which they laughed uproariously. One little girl with a long black ponytail bought me a wooden pig at one of our stops. She must have spent her food money for the day on it, because I didn't see her eat after that. It rained most of the two days but started clearing up when we reached Kangding, our last stop before we entered the closed area on the Chinese side of the Yangtze River.

Kangding was open to foreigners now, but definitely off the beaten path, and there were only a few hardy backpackers there. At the bus station we saw two women from Ireland who looked dazed and complained about the altitude, but they pointed us toward the only hotel. An American man wearing a North Face jacket and a long beard spotted us from across the street and bounded over to meet us. He introduced himself as Ethan Goldings, and his enthusiastic friendliness was unexpected and refreshing. That night over dinner and beer we exchanged stories and experiences. An anthropology major, Ethan had studied Chinese in China and Tibetan in India. His fluency in those two languages plus his ability to climb had gotten him on numerous expeditions in Nepal, Bhutan, and India, including one Everest expedition. Right now he was here to guide another American expedition to the east face (or Tibetan side) of Everest. He had flown to China a few weeks earlier to start making arrangements and to visit old friends. For us, he had a lot of good information about Tibet and some great topographic maps of Sichuan Province. As we talked, a deep rumbling in my gut clued me in that I was getting sick. Pascal seemed to be getting it too. Later that night I got a fearsome case of diarrhea, and by morning my legs were exhausted from the all-night battle with Chinese "squatter" toilets.

The next day I was weak and tired, although somewhat better. Pascal, however, took a turn for the worse, developing a fever and a sore throat, so he started a prescription of antibiotics and went to bed. There was nothing more we could do until he was well enough to travel.

Sophi and I tried to make good use of the time. One day we took one of Pascal's Nikon cameras and hiked high up into the heavily forested mountains above Kangding to visit Buddhist monasteries. Along the way I asked Sophi to tell me a little about herself.

"My father is Chinese and my mother was French," she said. "I was born in Beijing, China, and lived there until I was seven. Then we moved to Geneva, Switzerland, and later to Paris, France."

"Do you think of yourself as French or Chinese?" I asked.

"I guess more than anything else I'm French, although in some ways I am still very Chinese. My mother passed away when I was fifteen, and it was really difficult for us because she was the center of our family. My father and I had problems understanding each other for a while after that, so when I was nineteen, I decided to go back to China and study Chinese. I stayed there for three years and it was wonderful. My roommate was from America and we got along great. My father and I wrote a lot to each other and that relationship improved also. But then came the tragedy in Tiananmen Square, and I had to go back to France. I started over again in a French university and I'm still studying Chinese. About all I have left is to write my thesis, and then I'll begin work, hopefully as a translator."

Then she told me how Pascal had recruited her. "One day I saw an advertisement from a French professional photographer who was looking for someone to translate Chinese or Tibetan on a trip to Tibet. Well, I had already decided awhile ago that I wanted to go to Tibet. Here, I thought, was an opportunity. So I called him."

Pascal had advertised that he specifically wanted a man, but he had interviewed Sophi anyway and explained to her the specifics of our trip. "He was very kind," Sophi told me, speaking of their first few meetings. "Step by step he went over everything that would be required of me, what our goals would be, and the possible dangers involved. I was impressed by his honesty, especially in telling me his reservations about having a girl along. I could tell he was really serious about this project."

Eventually Pascal had narrowed his choice for the trip down to two, Sophi and a male translator. He had written to me and we had agreed that he should take Sophi for a trial hike somewhere to see if she could deal with the physical difficulties. One weekend they had loaded down two backpacks and driven to the French Alps.

"He put all kinds of food in our packs so we would have enough weight, and we hiked hard for three days. The third night, as we were eating dinner, Pascal asked me, 'Sophi, what do you think about this project?' I wasn't sure yet what I thought, and he seemed a little disappointed, but you see, I had to tell him the truth. I couldn't say something I didn't feel yet, and I told him that too. I asked him what he wanted me to say, to which he replied, 'It would be good if you said yes.' Then he pulled out a bottle of champagne and opened it up. It was the last night of my test hike, and the mountains were so beautiful. We drank the champagne and afterward I knew that, if Pascal ended up choosing me, I would go. At first my father was resistant to the idea. He was concerned that I really didn't know Pascal well enough, but I was going for sure, and he knew it and I knew it. He accepted my decision after a short time and has been at peace with it." Listening to Sophi talk, I decided Pascal had made a good choice.

Later that week, while Pascal was still sick, Xiao Long, one of the young Chinese women who worked in our hotel, invited us to go with her and her boyfriend to a nearby town in the mountains where there were many hot springs. We hitchhiked there on a coal truck, ate at a friend's house, then soaked and swam for several hours in the hot water. Later we hiked back to Kangding together through the mountains on little goat trails that cut through the dense green foliage blanketing the foothills. Xiao Long and her boyfriend showed us edible plants, berries, and nuts, and we snacked the entire way back. They were both in their early twenties and wanted to get married, but her parents didn't approve of his situation. He was a fireman, and I guess relatively poor. When we were completely alone, they held hands shyly and asked Sophi and me to take pictures of them together.

Our fourth night in Kangding, September 2, was Xiao Long's birthday. That evening her boyfriend and a few other friends surreptitiously held a party for her in a little banquet hall on the third floor of our hotel, and we were invited. We ate pot stickers (cooked on an electric hot plate), sunflower seeds, and other indescribable Chinese snacks, and we drank soda pop and beer. Pascal still wasn't feeling 100 percent and was on the wagon, and it was amusing to see him initiate a toast clutching a plastic bottle of water. At first we had to be relatively quiet and keep the lights low while one of the girls kept a watch out for anyone who needed to be let into a room. In China, hotel guests are not issued keys, so there is always a young woman who opens the door and lets in the guests. However, after 10:00 P.M., whoever was in charge must have gone to bed or left for the night. Everyone suddenly relaxed and we turned up the lights. We sang songs, talked as best we could, and goofed around until 11:00, when Xiao Long's boyfriend brought out a birthday cake. After he lit all twenty-two candles, she blew them out as we sang "Happy Birthday" in Chinese, French, and English.

KANGDING WAS THE last city in which we could move about freely and buy things as we wished, so we purchased enough food for three days, along with many small Buddhist pictures, pins, and holy trinkets to use as gifts for Tibetans. We also bought wooden bowls for eating *tsampa*, a Tibetan staple food made from roasted barley flour and butter tea. Pascal thought we'd more likely be fed if we had the appropriate bowls. On our last day in Kangding we purchased our disguises—Chinese hats and coats—and put our backpacks in the grain sacks. Pascal's light brown hair, though, could be spotted from a hundred yards. In Hong Kong we had originally agreed that as a kind of bon voyage ritual, he and I would shave our heads in Kangding. This would solve the hair problem and also give us an added incentive not to fail early on in the trip, since we knew we would feel ridiculous traveling back through China bald and having to answer inquiries. But at the last minute Pascal decided his head was going to be too cold, so he backed out, and I surely wasn't going to do it if he didn't! He settled for a crew cut that could easily be hidden under a Chinese Mao cap. I had my dark brown hair trimmed Chinese style, then dyed jet black. It was more effective than I expected. When we stopped at the first store after the beauty salon, the lady peered suspiciously at me for several moments, then asked Sophi if I was a foreigner or just a funny-looking Chinese.

The morning after Xiao Long's birthday, we boarded a bus and headed for Batang, two days west. We stopped for the night in a little Tibetan settlement on one of the many tributaries to the Yangtze River. It was still early in the afternoon, and after a rest we went for a hike so Pascal could photograph the surrounding country. We were accompanied by Justin, a red-haired Englishman who planned to hitchhike to Lhasa. After walking for some time up a steep trail into the mountains, we passed a group of Tibetans carrying heavy loads of supplies on their backs. We greeted them and continued on. Later, when we had stopped to rest, a boy about ten from the group caught up to us. He carried a ten-pound sack of flour on his back and was dressed in an orange sweatsuit. I grabbed the flour and, after swinging the boy off his feet, gave him a piggyback ride for half a mile up the trail. He giggled but eventually indicated he didn't want to go any farther, I supposed because he wanted to wait for the rest of his clan to catch up. As we sat waiting, he put his hand into the pockets of his orange pants and, one by one, pulled out each of his treasures: a plastic jumbo jet, a little toy racing car that could be wound up by backing it up on the ground, and then a little cap pistol. Last of all, he pulled out a pack of cigarettes and lit up.

The rest of the group arrived a little later and one man, maybe the boy's father, was upset. He shouted at us and motioned for us to go down, as he berated the boy. The trail was cut into a steep cliff, so when they hadn't caught up to the boy after their rest, they must have become worried that he'd fallen over and they'd passed him by. The man finally settled down after a few minutes and became friendly.

We hiked back to a small Tibetan village and ate at a restaurant owned by a Tibetan family. The owners' younger daughter brought me to her room and showed me pictures of her older sister taken while she was attending college in Chengdu—a beautiful Tibetan girl dressed in Chinese clothes. Most of the pictures were taken at Emei Mountain, which I had climbed three years before. They were the only pictures the family owned, as they didn't have a camera.

When I walked back into the kitchen, there sat the girl herself, dressed in the same blue dress she had on in the pictures, and she was even wearing lipstick. The only one of the family fluent in Chinese, she spoke with the standard Beijing accent. I visited with them the rest of the evening, and when Pascal, Sophi, and Justin were ready to leave, Sophi told me the girl wanted me to stay and talk, and that they were leaving me for the night. They teased me, Justin winked, and then they left.

For several more hours I sat on a sofalike piece of furniture with the girls, who were fifteen and twenty-one, and their little niece, about eight months old. The girls took turns going to wait on customers and we all took turns holding the baby, whose pants lacked a rear panel. On the walls were beautiful Buddhist paintings and symbols. The electric lights were turned down low, and traditional Tibetan butter lamps gave off a soft yellow glow and slightly sweet aroma from one corner of the room.

My Chinese vocabulary was still very limited, but I enjoyed our conversation. After all the customers were gone, the father came to take me up to a guest room and I realized that Sophi actually *had* made arrangements for me to spend the night with these people. He led me up a steep ladder to the third floor of the house and deposited me in a small, new room paneled in rough pine boards, the pleasant aroma of which filled the room. A little black wooden dagger hung by a length of red string above the door, along with two pictures of Buddhist deities on either side of the frame. These were placed there to protect the family from demons and devils, Pascal told me later. If you are a devil in disguise and you try to enter the house, the dagger will fall on you.

I lay down on the little wooden bed in the center of the room and pulled the thick quilt over me. I couldn't relax, though. In the darkness it seemed as though the bed was pitching back and forth and I was falling. I kept thinking I heard tiny footsteps on the ladder outside, but I couldn't tell for sure if it was evil spirits or just sounds made by a rope blowing against the house. I tried to reassure myself, but the sense of apprehension deepened, and I wanted to get out. I flipped on the light, put my clothes on, turned off the light again, and crept down the ladder to the ground. As I walked past the back of the house, the door was open and the whole family was busy doing dishes and getting food prepared for the next day. The oldest daughter, still in her blue Chinese dress and matching hair ribbon, sat at a low wooden table and kneaded dough into flat noodles. I watched her and the rest of the family for a few moments, then went back upstairs.

The next morning I felt very sick, but when I got back to the hotel I didn't tell the others. I decided it must be dysentery, and I started a prescription of antibiotics. I was sure I would be better by the time we started hiking in a few days, and I didn't want to worry Pascal unduly. No matter how much I insisted that nothing had happened, though, the others teased me endlessly about spending the night with the girls.

That day the bus climbed higher and higher onto the Tibetan plateau. Large square houses made of rock with three-tier roofs dotted the flat areas. Later I found out that this was a standard shape for Tibetan houses, though the materials from which they were built varied widely according to what was available. As we climbed higher, the Tibetan houses disappeared completely, and I saw my first yaks, great hairy beasts with shaggy tails. We could also see the yak-herders' tents, most of which were made of black woven yak hair, although a few were white canvas, indicating the advance of technology even among these simple people. We negotiated a 15,000-foot pass, then stopped for a break. Gongga Shan and other 22,000-foot peaks rose like fortresses in the distance from which we had come.

That evening we arrived in Batang. The town was still officially closed, but we met several other foreigners who said they had not experienced much trouble from the police. When we checked into a small hotel we were told by the staff that the police would be by to interview us later on, just to make sure we were heading back out of South Sichuan, not into Tibet.

Here we planned to cross the Yangtze River and enter Tibet, directly and illegally, by hiking into the mountains. We would hike through the Lake Bon region, where there are many nomadic Tibetans with yak herds, and in two weeks arrive at the Lancang River basin. Sophi asked around and found that even though there were check stations on each side of the bridge, both were manned by Tibetans and not by police. In China we'd found that the military, police, and civil authorities were distinctly separate and often didn't cooperate. Sometimes it was impossible to determine who had the final say or to predict how a particular official would react to or uphold the law. Although Tibetans are sometimes given positions of authority in the civil service, police, and military, they were often more resistant to the central Chinese authority and, we figured, more likely to be helpful to us. Sophi found a man with a truck who, for an extremely high price, would drive us into Tibet as far as Markam, about seventy miles. He said he knew where the police road checks were and that he would let us off so we could walk around them on foot. Markam is where the Sichuan-Tibetan highway and the Yunnan-Lhasa road join into a common road that eventually leads to Lhasa. It had gotten to be the stud thing among backpackers like Justin to try to hitchhike to Lhasa on trucks. Some actually made it. The police had found it easier to have one checkpoint where these two roads meet; from here they could catch travelers coming from either Sichuan or Yunnan, fine them, and send them back to China.

Pascal rationalized that because it was not uncommon for foreigners to be traveling illegally here, we probably wouldn't raise any serious suspicion if we were caught, and at worst we would get fined and sent down the Lancang toward Yunnan, which was exactly the direction we were headed anyway. If we made it successfully to Yanjing near the Lancang, we would cut ninety miles of hiking and about ten days out of our journey. This, Pascal contended, would give us a much greater chance of making it into the Drung valley. We would still spend two to three months in Tibet, just not so much time with the nomads, as we had originally planned. He was very convincing.

Then he suggested one more alteration in our carefully laid plans. Originally he had proposed crossing the Nu Mountains high above the Irrawaddy valley, which meant going ten days or more through an area where he believed no people lived. We would cross 18,000-foot passes through an arc of snowy peaks that spring from the divide between the Nu and Brahmaputra rivers, enclosing the headwaters of the Irrawaddy. I had thought it a bold proposition when he sent me a fax of the plan, but of course I was all for it. The high passes were what I had hoped for. Now he wanted to find somewhat lower passes further down on the Nu River. "You must understand, Wade, we have very little information on either proposition. It will still be an adventure, I promise."

All very logical, but I sensed it was happening again: on our first trip, two years ago, when we had tried to cross the mountain between the Lancang and the Nu River, the locals had told Pascal that the way was impossible, even though I felt we could make it over the passes. He had argued vehemently until finally I had given in and we had gone around and gotten arrested. The time we had lost had cost us the trip. I told Pascal now that I had sacrificed six months of my life and gone through some difficult decisions in order to be here and I wasn't willing to fail again unnecessarily. If it came down to it, I wanted it agreed that my decision would carry weight over any local advice when it came to crossing the mountains into the Irrawaddy valley. Pascal seemed surprised at how upset I was and told me that of course he trusted my judgment, that on our first trip he had only known me for a few days and wasn't convinced of my competence. He assured me of his goal to reach the Drung valley and that he was putting everything he had into it.

THREE

Yak Butter and Tea Dreams

THE DRIVE TO Markam lasted seven hours, including an hour's delay for a mud slide. It might have taken days to clear by hand, but shortly after we came upon the slide, an antique Chinese bulldozer chugged down the road, and soon our journey continued. Half a mile outside Markam the driver stopped and let us off, explained the location of the police check station, and then hurriedly left. We had done it! We were sixty miles inside Tibet, and it had been so easy. I thought back over the many elaborate plans we had made to get over the Yangtze, everything from building a boat to crossing at night on suspension cables, and I felt silly.

By entering Tibet illegally we joined a tradition of adventurers almost as old as the country itself. Extreme topography and Tibet's well-founded fear of Russia, China, and India have made it one of the hardest places to visit on earth. Tibet's official policy toward foreign visitors has almost always been "We don't want any." Volumes have been written on the many attempts by Westerners to sneak into Tibet—perhaps the most famous being Heinrich Harrer's description of his thousand-mile trek from India to Lhasa.

Less than a year after the revolution and the Communist victory, China announced its intention to "liberate" Tibet and invaded. Negotiations, effected under duress, led to the drafting of a seventeen-point agreement between the Tibetan government and China. To make the document appear official, the Chinese even forged the Dalai Lama's personal seal. Theoretically, Tibet became a regional "autonomous zone" of China, a kind of preserve, so to speak, with freedom of religion and protection of the traditional Tibetan culture. The reality was terror and oppression, and the Chinese became even more reluctant than the Tibetans had been to allow foreigners to visit and witness what was going on. Most of Tibet, especially the areas that border China, remains off-limits to foreigners.

We skirted the town, giving the police check station a wide berth, then rested by a stream. Sophi put on her Chinese hat, coat, and shoes and headed into town to buy food and gather information. She returned with biscuits, steamed bread, orange soda pop, and several cans of pork fat. We laid out a backpack as a table and had breakfast, after which we exchanged addresses and then said good-bye to Justin and the two German hitchhikers who had joined us to help pay the driver's exorbitant fee. The three of them had decided to team up for the rest of their trip to Lhasa. We hiked out of town and caught a truck heading south.

It took three days to reach Yanjing. The first night we camped well off the road in a beautiful little glen with grass cut short by grazing yaks. Several families of Tibetans came by at different times and watched us cook noodles and eat dried yak meat. We also boiled down and made crisps out of a couple pounds of pork rinds, pouring the resulting oil into the noodles to get our bodies used to a high-fat diet.

The next morning the Tibetans came again and helped us pack up camp. They were fascinated by our equipment and found such things as Velcro, Teva sandals, and hollow, lightweight tent poles strung with shock cords amazing. We stopped several hours at a Buddhist monastery so Pascal could photograph the inside, which had been mostly destroyed by the Chinese but now was slowly being rebuilt. The people living nearby brought us tea and were very friendly.

There was little traffic the second day, so we ended up walking a lot, finally catching a ride with a Tibetan man and his family driving one of the odd-looking "rototiller" tractors so common in China. Several times going uphill we stopped to drain the one-cylinder engine block of water and refill it from springs. There was no radiator. The Tibetans caught the hot water coming from the engine and used it to make tea. We stopped at the house of their friends or relatives to have tea made with yak butter and salt. This beverage, which is brewed from Chinese black tea leaves, several times a day is first boiled on a stove and then poured into a long, pipelike barrel made of slats of hardwood bound tightly with rawhide. Butter and salt are then added and thoroughly mixed in by forcing a wooden plunger on a long stick up and down several times inside the pipe. The steaming butter tea is then ladled into pots and placed on a tray, underneath which are smoldering hot coals. I drank five cups, surprised at how good I found it.

We were dropped off near the pass that led into the Lancang River valley. Pascal didn't trust several tough-looking Tibetans who were milling around, so we hiked a couple miles downhill and camped in a peaceful clearing protected from view by many pine trees.

Around 10:00 P.M. I was awakened by a soft clink of metal on metal. Unzipping the tent door, I dove out onto the wet grass, scrambled to my feet, and clicked on the hiker's headlamp I was holding in my hand. The beam revealed two rough-looking Tibetans in filthy sheepskin vests with long strands of red yarn wound in their hair. One was already running and the other stood holding our cook kit. He must have picked it up from the edge of the tent and then tried to tiptoe quietly away.

I shouted at the man and he set the pot carefully on the ground, then ran after his friend. I must have been quite a sight, standing there in my underwear. I crawled back into my sleeping bag and shivered for several minutes. We were above 12,000 feet and it was cold. I couldn't sleep the rest of the night, worried that the men, or others, might come again and try to steal something, even though we now had everything inside the tent with us.

AFTER THE YANGTZE, the Lancang was the second of the three major Tibetan rivers that we would have to cross in order to reach the Drung valley. The third was the Nu, or Salween, as it's referred to by the British. All three of these rivers originate on the great frozen plateau of north-central Tibet. As these rivers converge to roll through the mountains, breaching the great divide east of the Himalayas, they flow at one point within fifty miles of one another without joining. The country was very different from Yunnan, where Pascal and I had crossed over two years before. It was steeper, with 18,000- to 24,000-foot glacier-covered peaks rising almost vertically from the western banks of the Lancang.

Here all the houses were classic Tibetan: made of mud bricks, then plastered over and whitewashed. There was terracing here too, but nothing approaching the vast, stair-caselike fields we had found further down on our first trip.

We finally caught a truck ride most of the way to Yan-jing. It was absolutely full of Tibetans, bundles of supplies, and animals, but we jumped on anyway. There was a yak in the very back, and Sophi was stuck with its head in her face and lap for the entire ride. By the time we got off, she had yak drool all over her coat and pants. I didn't fare much better. The same yak kept shifting his weight each time we rounded a corner, and he invariably stepped on my feet. My cries of pain and Sophi's exclamations of disgust had the owner of the yak and the other Tibetan passengers roaring with laughter. But no one made any attempt to remedy the situation.

At Yanjing we had to be careful again of police, who were usually stationed where there was a fairly large population. We also needed a little time here to try to find a guide who would take us across the mountain to Bitu, our next destination.

Pascal had a lot of information on an old French Catholic mission that had once been in this area. He believed there were probably still practicing Catholics here and hoped they would take us in. We had seen a graveyard several miles back in which there were crosses. That would be a good place to start, he decided, so we asked a boy driving a rototiller to take us back there. The graveyard was fairly new, reconstructed in 1987, but many of the headstones were quite old. Pascal spent hours photographing the graveyard and headstones and had Sophi translate the Chinese captions into French so he could write down information important to the article he planned to write. Among the tombs was that of a Grand St. Bernard, who was a Swiss missionary and died there in the early 1900s.

Later we met an old wrinkled Tibetan man and Sophi asked him to take us to the church, even though we weren't sure if one still existed. He led us through a thick wooden gate into a little walled community, where we met three ladies dressed in traditional Tibetan clothes but wearing crucifixes. They looked to be in their seventies or eighties. After greeting us warmly, they took us to a large, white-washed building, where above the door were written Chinese characters I recognized to be the symbols for "Catholic." One of the ladies unlocked the door and in we went. The interior of the church looked new, in contrast to the rest of the building. The front part was dominated by a twelve-foot painting of Christ with the heads of six of the apostles floating above Him on the main altar. There were two small altars on either side, one for Mary and another for a saint none of us knew.

We photographed the interior, then went outside to visit with a small throng of people who had gathered on the steps to see the strange foreign visitors. There were eight small children, three old men, and seven or eight very old women. Only one man and his wife were anywhere near our age. All the people spoke some Chinese as well as Tibetan, and with Sophi's help we learned that the mission was founded in 1865 by French monks. It had survived and at times even flourished for eighty years. The French Roman Catholic Church had trouble finding priests willing to live in this and other missions here, so they petitioned the Monastery of St. Bernard in Switzerland for help. They knew the priests there were used to living high in the Alps and might better withstand Tibet's harsh winters. The

Monastery of St. Bernard assented, and eight priests were sent, one of which came to Yanjing. Then in 1946 all foreign missionaries were expelled by the Tibetan government and the church continued to run itself without outside help. From 1966 to 1975, after China's occupation of Tibet—or "liberation," depending on your politics—the Cultural Revolution raged through China and Tibet. The church was burned from the inside, and the people were forbidden to practice their religion. In 1987, when the Chinese government again allowed freedom of religion, the church interior was rebuilt. The original thick earthen walls and roof had survived the fire and were now one hundred twenty-eight years old.

AS SOON AS Pascal realized there was an active church here, he quickly put away his Buddhist pennants and became Saint Szapu. "Damn, I forgot my crucifix! I meant to buy one in Hong Kong," he lamented, as he practiced crossing himself. Pascal could change faiths about as effortlessly as most people can change their shirt. I had never really talked to him about it, but I always wondered what he really *did* believe. Personally, I felt a twinge of guilt at each of his deceptions, yet I couldn't deny that the more earthy part of me secretly admired and even yearned to emulate him.

As we visited with the people, they brought us wine and corn liquor to drink, but no one offered food or lodging, both of which we desperately needed. The population here was too dense for us to set up our tent without drawing attention and, inevitably, the police. We needed someplace to hide.

Pascal had me bring out pictures he had photocopied

from old books. They showed this area in the 1940s, when the church and mission were being operated by the French and Swiss priests. I had laminated these pictures in Hong Kong, and we now gave them out as presents. This impressed the people, and the old lady who had brought us the corn liquor filled our glasses repeatedly. Pascal, always respectful of my decision not to drink but mindful also of the necessity not to refuse hospitality, would drink for both of us—each time we set our glasses down, he would pick up mine and I his. We drank and visited, but still no one suggested that we stay the night. Finally Pascal had Sophi bluntly ask them. Sophi looked a little uncomfortable, but she did as he said.

The old lady took us to a large, ancient, wooden building behind the church where the missionaries had lived decades ago. It was an elaborate structure, three stories high in the back and one story high in the front, with an open courtyard in the middle. Most of the rooms were abandoned and filthy, but on the second floor small, cell-like cubicles still had doors and were being used. Someone else was already living there, but the old ladies merrily and unceremoniously scooped up all their things and carted them back down the stairs. Again I could see by the look on her face that Sophi was troubled by this. One of the kind old ladies brought clean blankets and linens for us to sleep on; then they all slipped off to evening prayer service.

Only twelve people attended the ceremony. There were no priests or leaders of any type. Three old men sat at the back of the chapel and the nine women scattered out toward the front. They recited prayers together for an hour, occasionally glancing over their shoulders to see if Pascal and I were still kneeling in the back at our pews. We later learned that this congregation met twice a day, seven days a week, and that a priest came only once a year from Yunnan to hear confessions and conduct Mass.

After the prayer service, several of the old ladies, the children, and the younger man and his wife came to visit us in our room. The couple brought two bottles of red wine. I noticed Pascal had switched his good watch with the altimeter and thermometer for one of the cheap ones he had brought along. After the lady gave us the wine, he acted deeply touched. I even thought I detected tears in his eyes. Looking as though he was going through a difficult deliberation, he finally seemed to make up his mind. Hesitantly he unbuckled the watch, then presented it to the lady. She wouldn't accept it, of course (who would have, after all that?), but he insisted, pressing it into her resistant hands and closing them over it. If I hadn't known differently, I would have believed Pascal had just given up his most prized possession, and that's what the lady must have thought because she burst into real tears, dropped to her knees, and clasped both his hands in hers.

WE WEREN'T OFFERED food, but after asking were shown to a kind of kitchen with an earthen stove and firewood. Here we were able to cook the noodles and dried yak meat we had purchased in Kangding. During dinner the husband and wife and one of their five children sat and visited with us. Through Sophi's translation, Pascal explained that we wanted to cross the mountains to Bitu and that we needed to find a guide and horses to carry our things through the high passes. The man told us he would do his best to find something, and he even thought maybe he could guide us himself.

A policeman came by during the evening, but Pascal spotted him before he saw any of us and warned us to stay out of sight. Whether he had heard that some foreigners were around and was looking for us or whether he was just a devout Catholic, we didn't know. No one in the monastery betrayed our presence, and we saw him leave a short time later. Our biggest concern here was the police, for if we were caught and our film confiscated, the trip would be over. We felt we could probably stay here safely at most only a day or two.

In the early afternoon the next day a small Tibetan man wearing a leather hat arrived in our room. He spoke Chinese and introduced himself as Zhong Xi, saying he had mules and would be willing to guide us to Bitu. We negotiated the price: four hundred yuan for the four-day trip, which was a little less than twenty American dollars a day. With mules, weight would no longer be an issue, so we decided to buy seven more days' worth of food in Yanjing for the trip into the Nu valley. Again Sophi put on her Chinese shoes, coat, and hat, and we hiked several miles to the city. While Pascal and I hid behind a stack of logs on the edge of town, Sophi went in and purchased the food: four pounds of noodles, ten pounds of rice, tins of beef and pork fat, candy, eight bottles of beer, four bottles of pop, and, of course, a carton of cigarettes. We carried the supplies back to the security within the walls of the old mission.

Zhong Xi later came by to tell us the weather was changing and that if it was raining in the morning, we wouldn't start. We told him we needed to go regardless. Too many people had seen us out and about. Depending on how on the ball they were, it would be only a matter of time before they would find our whereabouts and come investigate. We would have a hard time explaining all the food and equipment, let alone our presence in the closed area.

Again I attended the early prayer service, this time with Sophi, and by now I'd learned the pattern. At 6:30 in the morning a seventy-three-year-old lady dutifully walked up the steep stairs to the third floor of the mission, went out on the roof, and with a thick stick of apple wood rapped an old tire drum that hung by a rope. It sounded like a gong. Presumably there was once a proper bell here. Within fifteen minutes, seven or eight women between sixty-five and eighty and three old men gathered in front of the church. The youngest of the ladies, a woman with a kindly face and soft eyes, unlocked the front door, and all the members filed in slowly, taking their customary places throughout the pews, and knelt down. Still another lady let herself through a small gate at the front of the main altar and lit two candles in front of the huge painting of Christ. For about an hour and a half they recited prayers together and sang hymns; then they all wordlessly rose and left. The lady who had lit the candles went up and extinguished them with a little silver candlestick snuffer, and the same lady who had unlocked the door locked it again. Then came the interesting part: no jabbering, no gossiping, not any of the small talk one would expect. No, just a serene look in their eyes as they all filed quietly down the steps and went their separate ways. It was exactly the same with the evening service.

"SHIT, SHIT," PASCAL greeted the morning, as we stood in the doorway staring at the deluge of water pouring down from the gray heavens. "We must convince him to leave today. Maybe I'll offer more money."

Suddenly, at 8:00 A.M., an hour before we had expected him, Zhong Xi arrived at the gate with four mules and his sixteen-year-old son. He made no explanations as he hurriedly tied our bags to three of the pack saddles. We had an emotional parting with the old women. They obviously had very little extra of anything, and I knew we had caused them hardship and maybe even some risk by staying there, yet they had shown us great kindness. I felt deep pangs of guilt for deceiving them by pretending to be Catholic and I could see that Sophi was unhappy about it too. She glared at Pascal as she handed the women money, although it was difficult to get them to accept it. Each of them came forward and gave us a kind of hug where they touched their foreheads to our shoulders; then we left.

Yakalo, the little village in which we had been staying, was about two miles upstream from Yanjing, a good-sized city. In order for us to cross the Lancang River, we had to follow the road through Yanjing and then travel another mile or so downriver to the only bridge. There was no other way. We walked along nonchalantly, although inside I felt tense. We passed through the edge of the city without incident, but on the south end of the town was a check gate. A Chinese man sitting on some steps outside the booth saw us, jumped up, took two steps forward, then gawked at us before running back into the building, where he remained as we walked on.

As we crossed the Lancang and started climbing into the mountains, Zhong Xi insisted that Sophi ride the extra mule. When we reached the same elevation as Yanjing on the other side, we stopped at a large, very new Tibetan house. Zhong Xi opened the door to a kind of barnyard in front of the house and yelled. Soon we were led into the yard and then into the bottom floor of the house, mules and all. We took off the packs and saddles and rubbed the mules down. This was my first time inside a Tibetan house. The ground floor is where the animals are kept, and pigs, chickens, goats, and mules scattered out of our way as we walked to a steep set of stairs. We climbed to the second floor, where Zhong Xi introduced us to his younger sister and brother-in-law and several children. I was not sure which children belonged to the house and which were neighbors. This was where the people lived, along with a few young goats and chickens (but not piglets) that were allowed to spend their childhood with the family. When they were big enough not to be squashed by the other critters, they would be sent downstairs. As far as I could tell, the third floor was solely for the storing of hay, grain, and whatever else needed to be stored.

We stayed several hours with the family while it rained. Zhong Xi's younger sister fixed us a good, very filling meal of fried potatoes, squash, peppers, rice, and lots of butter tea. It is unbelievable how much of this drink an average Tibetan consumes at one sitting! The meal was more Chinese than Tibetan, but it was delicious. Zhong Xi's brother-in-law looked in a book, some sort of Tibetan almanac, and told us it was going to rain for the next few days.

Nevertheless, when the weather finally let up after several hours, we again saddled up the mules and headed back into the mountains. We trudged on for five hours straight in sporadic rain, gaining three thousand feet of elevation before finally stopping at a settlement of three large Tibetan houses occupied by five families. Everyone was shocked to see us arrive. Little children stopped what they were doing and came out to stare. We were the only foreigners any of them had ever seen, which was also true for most of the adults.

Zhong Xi went to the outer yard and yelled as before, and a short time later a young man around twenty opened the heavy wooden gate and let us in. We unpacked the mules and went upstairs, where we found eight adults in what could be called the "kitchen-dining-living area," a room dominated by a large, square clay oven with a circular opening in the front and several cooking holes in the top. Pots were placed on these cooking holes and smoke escaped around the pots to go through a hole in the roof. There was no chimney. The clay stove was so thick the top of it barely felt warm, even with a blazing fire. To one side of the room was a long, low table and deeply padded benches to sit on. Built into this table were metal urns, where glowing coals from the fire smoldered. The tops had round grooves holding pots of simmering butter tea. Also found on the table were large wooden bowls of roasted barley flour, which, mixed with butter tea, made tsampa.

Thick hand-sawn floorboards had been covered with half a foot of clay to make the floor fireproof. I figured the floors must be easy to repair: just get them wet, smooth them out, and make sure no one steps on them until they dry. The walls were also made of thick clay and were whitewashed on the outside. The roof was not held up by the walls but by massive log pillars about every ten feet throughout the structure.

The same young man who had let us into the house took us into an adjoining room and showed us three beds. They were covered with layers of yak hides and cow and sheep skins, along with wool blankets, which he stripped off and carried into the kitchen. Again we were taking someone else's beds. The boards of the bed were rough, and I was afraid they would puncture our air mattresses, so I asked for some old burlap bags to put under us.

Many people from the neighboring houses came and watched us set up for the night. As before when we had camped, our possessions fascinated them. They especially got a kick out of our headlamps. Whenever we pointed them at a child, he would throw up his arms and dash away giggling. Everyone took turns coming up and pressing down on our inflated mattresses, all the while exclaiming to one another.

As we cooked our dinner of noodles and tinned beef, I noticed that Zhong Xi and his son also ate food they had brought themselves. This seemed odd to Pascal, whose experience was that Tibetans usually fed even strangers until they were about to burst. The head of this household was Zhong Xi's brother. My guess was that Zhong Xi came this way regularly and probably stayed here so often that if he ate the family's food all the time, it would be a burden.

When I went out to relieve myself, I heard someone playing a harmonica in one of the other houses. I investigated and found several teenagers. They shyly waved me in and I played "O, Susanna," "When the Saints Come Marching In," and "Home on the Range" for them. They in turn played Tibetan songs and asked me to dance. I tried, but they laughed until I thought they would pass out. Later in the evening all the children from the three houses, about a dozen, came into the main room of the central house and started milling about. The young man who had let us in rosined up a bow and got out a Chinese instrument that had two strings and sounded a great deal like a violin. The children made a circle around one of the pillars, the girls on one side holding hands and the boys on the other side with arms clasped around one another's shoulders. The fiddler began to play and someone accompanied him on the harmonica while the children danced around in a circle. It reminded me of American square dancing and old-time fiddle music. The fiddler played a complicated piece of music for five or six minutes, then suddenly, perfectly on cue, the children began to sing. First the boys sang a deep throaty verse, then the girls sang an answering verse, and then the boys sang the next verse which the girls again answered. It was beautiful. I'd always thought of Asian music as drab and dissonant, and I hadn't expected anything like this. Pascal was also excited. He set up slave flashes and took picture after picture. He had an infrared sight on his camera like a laser sight on a rifle, so all he had to do was put the red dot on whatever he wanted to photograph, then press the button. His Nikon F4 automatically focused, adjusted the flash, and took the picture.

After several hours of singing, the head of the house, Zhong Xi's brother, who was ill, sent the children to bed. Earlier in the evening Zhong Xi had asked his brother if there was anything we could do for him. When I had examined him, I'd found his glands were swollen and he had a slight fever. Pascal had given him some medicine, making an exception to a rule we had agreed upon: not to give medication to anyone. We were afraid that if someone became worse afterward, we might be held responsible.

Zhong Xi was the only Tibetan who could speak Chinese, so there had been a little confusion when he had asked me to examine his brother. I'd started the examination, under the impression that Zhong Xi's brother had the flu. Then Sophi got the translation correct. Zhong Xi had actually told us his brother had been diagnosed with lung cancer in a Chinese hospital and asked if we had medicine that would make him well. I explained through Sophi that we could do nothing for him, that I couldn't even do a chiropractic adjustment for fear the cancer might have weakened the bones of his spine. His children were young, and I wondered if they had any idea how sick their father really was.

I DREAMED OF my father. I was hunting with him. We spotted a huge buck feeding from across a canyon. The wind was right, and it carried a trace of the deer's musk. Pausing briefly, I levered a shell into the chamber of the .270 and snapped the bolt shut before cautiously advancing over the ridge. Nothing! He'd outfoxed us. I sighed and relaxed. It was like Dad had said: "It's usually no accident they survive long enough to get that big." A flicker of movement caught my attention. I pulled the gun to my shoulder and through the 9X power scope, the tiny insectlike figure became my father standing silhouetted between the sky and the bald granite mountain from which he had sent me. Waving his arms frantically, he pointed down to the canyon below. Puzzled, I lowered the rifle and looked again, but there was nothing—except for a scrubby patch of stunted buck brush. No deer in its right mind would hide in there. Again I looked through the scope to my father. Now he was jumping up and down, gesturing wildly and still pointing toward the thin patch of brush. He suddenly froze, extended the first finger on his right hand, and cocked back his thumb. Understanding the gesture, I quickly drew my pistol, bracing the rifle on my thigh as I'd been taught, and fired three quick rounds into the small green patch. Nothing stirred. I reholstered the pistol and started walking casually toward the point where I had just fired, convinced now that Dad had been mistaken. Suddenly the tiny patch of brush exploded into motion, as the massive beast erupted from the foliage and began bounding downhill at tremendous speed. As if of its own volition, the gun flew to my shoulder. At the same instant the trophy head appeared in my scope and I fired. The five-point rack jerked to one side. Twisting in midair, the buck plunged antler-first into the rocky hillside, then slid to a rolling halt several yards below. I leaped down the hill, grabbed the head by the antlers, and drew my knife. A long, drawn-out scream echoed through the mountains. I paused, opened my throat, and let my voice join that of my father's in the primeval cry of triumph, and when my lungs were empty, I reached down with a quick slash and cut the throat.

Now I awoke with a start, muscles tense, heart beating wildly as it pounded blood through my head. "Too much butter tea," I mumbled. I got up and went to relieve myself. I wondered why I had dreamed about shooting the big buck. The dream had been lucid, the details perfect, exactly as the event had occurred in the summer of my fifteenth year. But it had been years since I had even thought about hunting. It was something I didn't think about by choice. The sudden intrusion of this memory into my dreams disturbed me, as had the vision of the jackrabbit back in Hong Kong. Why was I thinking about these things that were better left buried?

Making my way back to the bed, I paused for a moment and looked down at Sophi, who had wiggled partway out of her bag and now looked cold. Her smooth skin was delicately lit in the moonlight that filtered through the wooden shutters. The ice and steel she wore by day had melted away and she appeared soft and vulnerable in sleep. Gently I pulled her sleeping bag to her chin and rezipped it. She stirred and turned her head to one side but didn't awaken. I quickly pulled my own sleeping bag back around me and shivered until I was warm, then, still exhausted from our first real day of hiking, quickly fell back to sleep and into a darker dream in which my Tibetan pony reared in fright, then broke into a full-out gallop as he emerged from the shallow canyon and onto the open plateau. His soft brown eyes strained wide, glazed with fear, the rale of his breath whistled in and out past the heavy bronze bit that held the reins I clenched in my fist. The animal was small, yet heavily muscled, and surprisingly surefooted as he rocketed over the uneven, stony ground. I was riding without saddle or stirrups, my legs tightly clamped around his naked sides as I frantically fought to stay balanced and in rhythm with the animal's frenzied stride. Through the surrealistic dreamscape, I saw ahead two white, ice-covered mountains, between which was a narrow notch. Somehow I knew if I could just hold on until we reached that point, I'd be safe, I'd be free. But suddenly a dark shadow swept across the plateau, intercepting our path, and the horse beneath me began to gallop even faster. Darkness gathered around us as the shadow condensed and became more defined, revealing itself as the silhouette of a huge hovering bird. Clamping my legs tighter, I yearned to look back, but knew if I tried I would certainly lose my balance and tumble to the rocky earth below. The pass loomed ahead, but I knew in my gut I was never going to make it. A shrill cry came from above, then the rapidly increasing sound of rushing air as I crouched in terror, waiting for the impact.

WE AWOKE AT 6:30 and ate a meal of tsampa with Zhong Xi and his son. Up, up, up we climbed, following a steep river valley through a forest of large conifers I had not expected to find in Tibet—some of the fir trees were five and six feet in diameter at the base. It was wonderful to have our packs carried. Pascal and I were free to take pictures, and without the weight, we could enjoy the incredible scenery. At a small meadow where we ate lunch, we found two caravans of traveling merchants and shared their fire. Zhong Xi fixed us a lunch of tsampa, butter tea (which he mixed by twirling a branch inside a tea pot), red hot peppers, raw pork fat, a little dry yak cheese, and three round loaves of Tibetan corn bread. The mules got grain in little sacks hung from their necks.

We loaded up the animals and continued our climb out of the valley. The tree line was at 12,000 feet, and we climbed to nearly 15,000 feet according to our altimeter before reaching the pass. Zhong Xi insisted that Pascal and Sophi ride the mules the last thousand feet or so. He even rode one himself, but I wanted to take pictures, so I continued walking. The poor mules must have been beat, carrying double loads at that altitude, but they puffed along at the same pace they had kept the whole day and I was hard put to keep up with them on foot.

The pass through the Nu Mountains was a desolate place marked by a huge rock cairn supporting hundreds of poles with prayer flags flapping in the wind. Only the lichens and a few hardy bushes could survive at this altitude, and gray jagged peaks towered above us on both sides of the notch.

FOUR

Change of Plans

THE NEXT MORNING in Bitu, Zhong Xi came in to say good-bye. He gripped both of my shoulders, squeezed them hard, and gave me a toothy smile. Just that morning I had learned from Sophi that Zhong Xi was the son of the old white-haired lady who rang the tire-drum bell each day for the prayer service back in Yakalo.

In the early afternoon, two village officials, Da Xi and La Ba, fixed us lunch and then took us to the ruins of an old monastery. They had not been happy to see us but nevertheless treated us with generous hospitality out of politeness. Da Xi told us we were the first foreigners to visit since 1988, when three English travelers had arrived. No other foreigners had come to Bitu since before the revolution. The walls and roof of the monastery were still intact, but the inside was gutted. Everything had been violently broken by the Red Guards. Before the Cultural Revolution, Bitu was a monastery city, home to over a thousand monks; common people were allowed in only during the day for worship. The city had a high stone-and-earth wall around it, and at night, all the common people were expelled and the three gates securely barricaded. During the Cultural Revolution, the Red Guards broke down the walls and destroyed the monastery and many of the houses. Most of the monks were able to flee to India, but as in other parts of Tibet, some were forced to renounce their religion and go to work as peasants.

This monastery was over three hundred years old, and as we walked through the abandoned, broken rooms, La Ba told us they were planning to rebuild. He anticipated the work would start in three years. He said the town itself was filled with ghosts, but nonetheless, after the monastery had been destroyed, common people had taken over, repaired, and occupied the homes left by the fleeing monks. Many beautiful wood carvings had survived the ravishing of the Red Guards, and we spent time photographing them. In one room we found a picture of Mao Tse-tung. Yellow and faded, it remained plastered on the wood banister where the Red Guards had placed it over thirty years before. I was surprised no one had removed it and decided maybe they had left it there as a reminder of the horrors of the time. We also visited a new monastery being built in the middle of town. It was going to be huge when finished. I wondered where they got the manpower to work on the thing, as I had hardly seen anyone around.

When we returned to the guest house, La Ba took me to his room and showed me a photo album with a few pictures of his family and friends, but mostly of his time in the military. He had served in the Chinese People's Liberation Army in Lhasa for four years. Next, he brought out his most prized possession, a small stack of magazines with brown paper taped carefully over the covers. Dirty books? No, magazines about movies—and the paper was there to protect the covers. We looked at them together for several hours, then La Ba went out to collect mushrooms, which he dried outside in the courtyard and sold to traveling merchants.

When the light was perfect, Pascal and I went on a "hunting trip," as he liked to call his photographic excursions. We hiked down and photographed the steep canyon walls of the Yuqu River, a tributary of the Nu River, and the outskirts of the small village. He had been very quiet the entire day. I wondered if there was some problem with his camera. "There are problems with Sophi," he finally said when I pressed him. They were not getting along well.

I decided to go back to my room and have a nap, but no sooner had I returned than Da Xi and a few other villagers arrived with a man they wanted me to examine. Twelve days before he had fallen from a horse and had not been able to move his neck or upper back since. At first I refused to work on him, because without X rays, I couldn't know where any fractures might be. He wouldn't leave, though, and just sat on one of the low benches we were using as beds and stared pleadingly at me. Earlier in the day I had worked on Da Xi's jammed wrist, and the day before had lanced an abscess on the hand of one of the merchants, so I guess word had gotten out. Da Xi told me this man was a close friend and asked me to please "fix" him because he couldn't work in his field the way he was. Again I refused, and the look of disappointment and pain in the man's eyes made me feel terrible. My Chinese was not good enough to explain adequately why I wouldn't work on the man.

"Where is Sophi?" Pascal asked when he came in. She and Da Xi had been gone most of the day and we had assumed they were together, but he was here now and still Sophi was missing. We asked Da Xi where she was. She is fine, he gestured, but he looked sheepish.

The man still wouldn't leave, so I finally decided to go ahead and work on him. I carefully adjusted him and did some acupressure, after which he thanked me graciously and hobbled out. I was just laying out my bed when one of the village men dashed into the room, his face ashen with terror. *"Sobi! Sobi!"* he shouted, pointing out the door.

Pascal jumped up. "Something is wrong with Sophi!" he yelled, and bolted for the door. I grabbed my first-aid kit and rushed after him. The man led us across the courtyard to Da Xi's room, all the time babbling in Tibetan.

Inside, we found Sophi half in bed and half hanging out over a metal basin, retching violently. The smell of alcohol and vomit filled the chambers. Pascal laughed in relief. "She's only drunk!" The Tibetan man looked at Pascal with surprise and fear. Da Xi entered the room a moment later and began apologizing. *"San ping! San ping!"* he kept saying, holding up three fingers to emphasize that he and Sophi had only drunk three bottles of distilled corn liquor. (The next day Sophi insisted it was only two, so either she had lost track after the second or Da Xi had miscounted.) We cleaned her up some and left her to sleep it off for a few hours.

Da Xi fixed us a wonderful dinner of mushrooms and rice. It was too bad Sophi wasn't conscious to enjoy it, because meals like these were fast becoming scarce. Mushrooms were the major cash crop here, and at this time of year everyone was out collecting and drying them to sell to traveling merchants.

Da Xi had promised to have a village dance for us that night, and the whole village showed up. We started a bonfire outside in the larger courtyard, and for several hours the Tibetans played their Chinese fiddles, sang, and danced in a circle around the fire. Later Pascal and I took Sophi and put her to bed in her own sleeping bag.

• • •

EARLY IN THE morning of September 14, just after I awoke, the man whose neck I had adjusted the day before appeared. He was visibly excited and showed me that he now had a little range of motion back. Through Sophi he told me that last night had been the first time he had slept since the injury. I adjusted him again and told him to come back that night. Several other people came by to be worked on. One old Tibetan lady had a frozen thumb joint and I was able to fix it in two adjustments. After that, whenever I saw her walking around town, she would hold up her hand and flex her thumb to show me it was still working.

Da Xi invited us to go for a hike with him in the mountains above Bitu. We climbed up a steep trail and soon came to some huge platforms of land that had been invisible from below. Only a small number of them were being cultivated, and when we asked why, Da Xi said there were not enough people anymore to farm all the good land available. The area had long since been deforested, but now there were new trees growing up. This tree-planting project was only three years old, and Da Xi explained that the Chinese had imposed a thousand-yuan fine for anyone caught cutting new trees.

We hiked on around the mountain, traversing the vertical cliffs by walking on the side of a newly built irrigation canal. Da Xi told us that this canal, about two miles in all, had been built by hand in twenty-nine days by over a hundred men. The Chinese government had sent in an engineer with a work order to build the canal. The increased water supply would supposedly improve production of crops, making Bitu more valuable to China. They allotted only five thousand yuan (about a thousand dollars) for the project, however, so much of the labor was done without pay.

Eventually we came into sight of a beautiful snow-capped mountain. It was formed of some type of coal-black rock, and its jagged, needle-shaped spires thrust up through the snow like splinters of ebony. On a rocky outcropping Da Xi paused and told us several legends of the mountain.

He said that there were only seven of these mountains in the world, all of them female. Those who were born facing them were wise and beautiful. Unfortunately this mountain had its back to Bitu, so the people there had always been ugly and stupid. He laughed at this, then continued. "In this area, there are three sacred lakes. If a person puts a plate of wood in one of the lakes, it can be found in one of the other two the following year, even though no rivers join the lakes. The most powerful of these lakes is found below the mountain we are looking at.

"When rain is needed, people sometimes go to the edge of the lake, where they shout and throw sticks and rocks into the water. It usually works. To get to the lake, you must pass through a thick, enchanted forest with trees so high and branches so close together it is like a night without stars, even during the day. Many things can be heard in these woods: voices of people, chickens, and other animals, but they are not really there." Pascal and I were intrigued and sorely tempted to go have a look at this lake for ourselves, but we agreed to stick to our goal of going to the Drung valley; afterward, we could do other things if we had time.

After telling his stories, Da Xi led us further into the mountains. Because it was harvesting season for barley, all the people were up on their roofs threshing. The barley is cut green and then carried to the roof and put under the eaves to dry. Next it is beaten with whip-sticks to knock the kernels from the heads. The threshing was done by groups of three, who sang as they worked. They would sweep the barley into baskets, to be sifted in the wind. Whoever was sifting whistled for the wind to come, and as soon as he whistled, a long, gentle gust would come along and carry the chaff away. When one scoop of barley was done, the wind would die down again. Then they would get the next scoop, whistle for the wind to come again, and it would. I watched one girl, about twelve years old, do this for an hour, and the wind came every time she whistled. Later this barley would be roasted and ground into flour for tsampa.

Everywhere we had stopped, Da Xi had helped with the work. Now I tried to help too, but my futile efforts to run the two-piece threshing sticks brought gales of laughter from the farmers. Even more distressing was my attempt at whistling for the wind. At first nothing happened, then a huge gust came and carried both chaff and barley off the roof. I am convinced it was coincidence, but the little girl scolded me soundly, and again everyone laughed. The people were kind to us wherever we stopped. They fed us fresh yak buttermilk and smoked yak cheese. Pascal also sampled *chang*, a Tibetan alcoholic beverage much like beer.

When we arrived back at the village, the man I had adjusted was waiting in our room. His hands were covered with mud and he had brought a bucket of potatoes and onions he had just dug as a gift for us. I adjusted him again and, while I was working on him, Pascal came in. "Wade, the police are here."

I finished up and was led to Da Xi's room, where Pascal and Sophi were already being interviewed. The Tibetan policeman was dressed in a clean blue uniform, which signified he was a public official. He had a gun.

Even though we knew he could speak Chinese, he

insisted on having La Ba translate for him. As we had agreed earlier, we refused to surrender our passports but instead presented photocopies of our passports and visas.

"Why are you here in this closed area?" he asked. "How do you French people know this American?"

Pascal replied that we had all met in Hong Kong and that his purpose for being here was to visit the ruins of a monastery in Menkung where his grandfather had been a French missionary. I stared at him in surprise. He told it with such emotion that I almost believed him. Sophi translated, but the policeman didn't bat an eye.

"What is the name of the monastery?"

Pascal looked at me and laughed nervously. Everyone looked on expectantly.

"So what is the name of the monastery?" I asked him.

"I don't know," he replied, "you know I am just making this up!"

"Man, Pascal, if you are going to lie, at least have your story straight," I said.

There were a few moments of tension, then suddenly the policeman exploded into laughter. He laughed and laughed with a kind of abandon only possible from a Tibetan. Pascal started laughing too and glared at Sophi and me out of the corner of his eye, motioning with his chin for us to join in. The man laughed until there were tears in his eyes and, when he could finally speak, he told us it was all right for us to go to Menkung—for whatever reason—and that was the end of our interview. Before he left, he told me he had heard I'd helped the sick people in the village, and he thanked me very sincerely. None of us ever figured out what had been so funny.

That night we tried to negotiate for some mules to

carry our things to Menkung. No one really wanted to go because it was harvest season, and the trip meant taking three days of fairly dangerous trail. Finally Da Xi found three mules and a young man named Zhu Mu, who said he was twenty but looked and acted more like fifteen. We bought dried yak meat and cooked some potatoes in preparation for the next day.

ZHU MU WANTED all the money for the trip up front. He didn't trust us, nor we him, and to make matters more difficult, he spoke only Tibetan, so it was impossible to communicate directly. We had to speak through Da Xi. We finally gave him one hundred yuan and agreed to pay 250 more when we arrived at Menkung. The entire village, including the man with the injured neck, showed up to watch us leave. We dropped into the Yuqu River and crossed on a narrow cantilever bridge. Next we climbed over a fin-shaped mountain that was almost an island where the river doubled back on itself. We traveled twelve hours, stopping only once for lunch at a small stream.

The further west we traveled, the wider and steeper the country became. By early evening we arrived in a small village a thousand feet above the Yuqu River. At the door of a large house, a man and his wife yelled down from the roof to greet us before Zhu Mu could yell up at them. In a minute they were helping us unload the mules and take our things to the second story. We were given a small room, where we quickly laid out our beds. The floor was rough-hewn planks, polished by years of people sleeping on them. The family watched in fascination as we blew up our air mattresses and unrolled the fluffy down sleeping bags from their tiny stuff sacks. They had to come touch everything. Then Pascal went out picture hunting and I climbed up onto the roof to watch the sun glisten on the glacier-covered mountains in the west.

The family had four children: one girl about seven, a boy about eight, a boy of five or six, plus a baby. The house was amazing. In America it would have been a lawsuit waiting to happen. The staircase, simply a log with notches cut into it, poked through a large square opening in the floor that had no guards or rails of any kind around it. The roof was flat and covered with clay, and although the family spent a lot of time there, again there was nothing to keep a little child from stepping off and getting mangled on the rocky ground thirty feet below.

As I was sitting on the roof, the young girl came teetering up the notched ladder, the baby strapped to her back with a length of old, frayed blanket. She was followed by her two brothers, who immediately began hounding me for more of some candy I had given them when we arrived. When I showed my pockets to be empty, the smallest boy became very aggressive, grabbed a stick from the woodpile, and waved it menacingly. His mother, hearing the commotion, came trudging up the ladder. She assessed the situation with a glance, let out a yell, and took off after the child, who dropped the piece of wood and ran for all he was worth to the edge of the building. At the last instant he veered left and ducked under his mother's outstretched arms; both of them came inches from running off the roof. He then doubled back, shot across the roof, and was just starting down the ladder when his mother caught him, dragged him back up, and paddled him soundly with the same stick he had threatened to use on me.

Zhu Mu roused us out of bed promptly at 6:00 A.M. I looked over at Pascal and almost screamed. The whole left side of his face was swollen badly, and his left eye was completely shut. "It's the flea bites," he lamented. There were big rows of bites all over his neck, face, and arms. Sophi had gotten bitten too, though not as badly, but Zhu Mu and I were mercifully spared. We quickly packed, cooked some noodles, and ate some of the family's rice for breakfast, then loaded the animals. I left some of our uncooked rice to replace what we had eaten, and we were off.

Zhu Mu was still somewhat reserved toward us, but around midday we overtook two boys who were about his age, and they decided to travel with us. Maybe Zhu Mu didn't feel so outnumbered, because suddenly he broke off the slow, forlorn dirge he had been chanting the whole time and with his friends began to sing livelier Tibetan tunes. We stopped at a small prayer house for lunch and cooked a large meal of tsampa, butter tea, and noodles. A nine-foot-tall prayer wheel dominated the middle of the room.

Tibetans never hobble or tie up their mules. One of the boys had warned us that his mule was dangerous and to be careful of it. He wasn't exaggerating. As we stood near the prayer house, suddenly and with no provocation his mule turned away from us, rocked onto its front legs, and let go with two flying kicks, one of which came inches from my face and the other of which struck me squarely just above the belt. I staggered back as the mule took two more steps backward and let fly with a second volley of kicks, again just missing my head. I stumbled away, and for a moment my temper flared. I felt like charging the beast. But I cooled down—my two money belts had absorbed much of the force of the kick, even though my stomach showed some ugly bruises for several days.

IN THE EARLY afternoon we set out again, climbing steadily out of the steep canyon of the Yuqu River. At 15,000 feet the topography became less extreme, and we passed through high U-shaped valleys, then entered a thick forest of firs and pines. The bottoms of the valleys had been cleared and homesteaded. Log cabins with smoke curling lazily out of rock chimneys and a backdrop of evergreens and rugged mountains looked more like frontier America than anything I would have expected in Tibet.

From the top of one 12,000-foot pass we could see the Nu River. It wound serpentinelike through dry canyon walls, bearing little resemblance to the slow, wide flow of muddy water it would become in Yunnan over a hundred miles downstream. We descended the slope and found pine trees with large cones, which we knocked down with rocks, then smashed open to obtain pockets full of pine nuts. The Tibetan boys sang gaily and laughed when we tried to sing their songs. Sophi and I in turn sang Billy Joel songs, and they tried to mimic us.

The mules ran ahead. When we caught up to them, we discovered that the two mules the boys had been riding had disappeared and only ours were there. The boys had to go back up into the woods to look for them, so we said good-bye and continued on, finally stopping for the night in the small village of Zena. Zhu Mu led us to a large house, where a father and son helped unload our mules. These must have been friends or relatives, because he obviously knew them well. We were taken through the barnyard and up the ladder to the living quarters, where the mother of the family brought us hot butter tea, tsampa, and squash fried in butter, along with balls of unleavened bread made of barley flour. We had been told by Da Xi that the water in Zena came from poisonous springs, and the people here confirmed we were not to drink it. Presumably they carried their water great distances, so we had nowhere to fill up our canteens for the next day.

After dinner, we climbed up onto the roof and set up our tent. Pascal wasn't about to offer himself again as cuisine for whatever vermin were living in the house below, and the inside of the tent was clean and bug-proof. The two or three families that lived in this large house gathered on the roof and watched in fascination as we worked. I tried to imagine how an American family would react if strange-looking foreigners who couldn't speak a word of English arrived and when offered the master bedroom, instead simply dropped their things on the floor, went to the roof, and set up a tent.

In the morning we slept in, even though Zhu Mu tried his hardest to roll us out at 6:00 A.M. But we'd put in two twelve-hour days of hiking and were exhausted. At 8:00, we finally got up and ate a meal of corn bread, greens, and butter tea one of the wives had set out for us. We gave the family money, which they accepted, and again started down toward the Nu River.

When we reached the high cliffs above the roaring white rapids, we turned north upriver, leaving the Pilgrims' Trail that led to the sacred Kar-Kar-Po Mountain. Pascal told me we were now on the main trade road to India, and if we continued on this trail, we would reach the China-India border in about ten days. As we descended into the canyon, a dramatic change took place. The climate became extremely arid and about the only vegetation were cacti that looked to be prickly pear. In another couple of weeks the fruit would be ripe. My mouth watered. Zhu Mu cut some of the fruit and ate it green. The larger cacti were over six feet high. A few yaks grazed the sparse grasses growing in infrequent clumps between the thick beds of cacti. On the hillside above, an amorous young bull, oblivious to our presence below, suddenly mounted a female yak that was staring nonchalantly at our small caravan. She bellowed in surprise, lost her balance, and came galloping down the hill, the bull still perched on her back, front legs clamped around her flanks and back legs pedaling to keep up. I yelled a warning to Sophi, who looked up just in time to leap out of the way and escape impalement by the two sets of horns being propelled by several tons of wriggling yak flesh. Later Pascal and I joked about having to explain to her father the strange manner of her death.

Eventually we reached a bridge and crossed the Nu River. After climbing two thousand feet up the other side of the valley, we arrived at the village of Menkung, perched above the Nu on a small plateau formed by an alluvial deposit just below the mouth of two canyons. Half a mile below the village gushed a white-water stream where at least ten water mills for grinding corn and barley were situated along the southern bank. As we entered the village, the people stopped what they were doing and followed us to where we unloaded the mules. Eventually a friendly man who spoke Chinese came by and told us he was the school-teacher for this area. He invited us to stay in the school building, a one-story U-shaped structure of single rooms, each having its own door. The front of the U was connected by a high stone-and-clay wall with a large wooden gate.

This formed a square courtyard in the center. The room we were given was absolutely filthy, but several children were assigned the task of sweeping it out with barley-straw brooms. Someone hauled a large bucket of water and wet down the rough plank floor. With an ax the teacher cut us a stack of kindling, lit a fire in the fireplace, then sent someone for a cast-iron pot stand so we could cook. We made up a large pot of noodles and ate, and also purified several quarts of water and drank our fill. The heat and exertion of crossing through the desert climate along the Nu River had taken its toll. All three of us were exhausted.

Only two men in Menkung spoke any Chinese, the schoolteacher and another man, who was the chief of the village. Both seemed very kind and brought things for us. As soon as we had eaten and rested a little, Pascal, through Sophi, started questioning the men about the possibility of crossing the mountains from here. This was maddening for me, because I could understand just enough Chinese to not quite get what was being said, and then of course I couldn't understand the French translation at all. The information was important to me because I wanted to cross the mountains high up in the Irrawaddy basin and I was sure the men were trying to talk Pascal out of the idea. Sophi had a hard time translating into French and English at the same time. Finally I forced myself to leave so they could finish the conversation without my interruptions. I stalked angrily out into the courtyard and began pacing back and forth on the dusty ground, waiting impatiently for them to finish.

In negotiations, I was at a distinct disadvantage, and right now I felt Pascal wanted it that way. When he had originally invited me to come on this second expedition, he had sent a detailed letter describing the route he intended to follow. From here we were originally to go north from Menkung up the Nu River, eventually crossing high mountain passes to the headwaters of the Irrawaddy. From that point we would travel downstream through very wild, in some places uninhabited, areas until we reached the head of the Drung valley, where the east and west forks of the Irrawaddy joined near the border of Burma. It was a bold and exciting proposal, and the prospects of completing this part of the journey were what had persuaded me to come. But almost from day one, Pascal had shown unreasonable pessimism about this plan. He argued energetically, plucking new reasons out of thin air and drawing the worst possible scenarios. Lately he had begun to insist that crossing high into the Irrawaddy had never been his intention, but just one of many possibilities he had considered, then rejected early on as being too dangerous.

When I saw the two Tibetans leave, I hurried back inside and asked Sophi to tell me what had gone on. "He says there is no need to cross the mountains," she reported. "In fact, he says, it would be dangerous and stupid to try. The Chinese have built a road, a major highway, in fact, from Gongshan into the Drung valley, and even now there is a bus that goes back and forth several times a week. He suggests that we go there and take the bus."

"Pascal! What is going on?" I shouted. I saw our entire adventure going down the drain. On our first trip, after dodging authorities the way we were doing now, I'd finally talked Pascal into bypassing the roadblocks and check points by crossing the ridge of mountains between the Lancang and Nu Rivers. He had hesitated when the weather turned bad, but then went along. After all, we had rain gear, warm clothes, and boots. Good grief, I'd wanted to say, this was only a 12,000-foot pass, not Mount Everest! I couldn't understand how someone who had such confidence in his ability to travel illegally in a Communist country could have such an irrational fear of the elements.

"Pascal, let's either go up or down," I'd said.

"Are you sure we can make it?"

"No, I'm not sure, but we will never know if we don't try. If worst comes to worst, we can always just come down. It's a mountain, not a black hole!"

He didn't answer. I got up angrily and began stuffing things into my pack.

"So, you are going by yourself?"

I stopped packing and looked straight at him. A slight hint of a smile touched the corners of his mouth.

ON THAT FIRST trip, we had slogged through the drizzle for four hours until we hit the snow line, and even though he was keeping up physically, I felt as though I were dragging Pascal behind me. He didn't have a positive thing to say about the whole idea. When we got to where the snow started, we came upon a broken house, this one made of rock. My heart sank. I knew that as long as we kept moving, maybe I could get us over the mountain, but now that there was shelter, it would be time for Pascal to stop, brew up a cup of coffee, and dig in his heels again.

"Look! A shelter. Let's rest and see if the weather will break for us. Can you get a fire going?"

It was already late morning, and as far as I was concerned, time was much more of an issue than weather. Alpine climbers learn to move fast, get up and get down quickly before the odds have time to turn against them, and that was my feeling here. Pascal, on the other hand, fought his wars by siege: go slowly, wait until the perfect minute, hour, day, month, year. Always have your retreat ready.

"Pascal!" I shouted through the rain. "There are two types of mountain climbers—those who hesitate and those who are still alive! Let's go for it, just this once!"

"You keep saying 'go for it' but I don't understand what you mean!"

So I had to explain "go for it," and he finally said, "O.K., I understand. Maybe you are right. Just let me rest a few minutes and give me a drink of water."

"Don't you have the canteen?" I asked.

"No. I gave it back to you after the last rest stop."

That was two thousand feet and probably a mile below us! As I clumped back down the mountain I thought sourly that I might as well have brought my pack down with me—giving Pascal two hours to think about going on through the snow in this weather would finish it for us.

I found the canteen beside where I had sat and trudged back up to where Pascal was waiting. There was an unlikely break in the weather, and I found him photographing some beautiful spring wildflowers with his 200mm macro lens.

"It is so beautiful with the rain on it!" he said intently as he clicked off several more exposures.

"What do you think about the mountain?" I asked halfheartedly, already dreading the answer.

Pascal snapped the massive lens off and put his camera away. "I have been thinking about what you said. I want to, as you say, go for it!"

We put on the fur-lined boots, hats, and other warm clothing we had brought with us. It felt great to get the weight out of my pack. Half a mile later one of my boots began to tear away, the leather disintegrating like wet cardboard. I took out my extra burlap gunny sack and loosely stitched it around my foot and leg like a moccasin and we continued. The clouds closed in, engulfing us. A thousand feet higher and the rain turned into light snow, which the wind blew furiously. We could see nothing, so I just followed the compass. There was no vegetation visible, just rock, snow, and clouds stretched out in a desolate, tilted wasteland of grays and whites.

Pascal seemed to have a little trouble with the altitude but didn't complain. Up, up, up, I had kicked steps in the snow and Pascal had followed. With no visual reference it had seemed endless, but finally we'd hit the pass—about five hundred feet up on the south side of the notch—but pretty good for going blind. The wind howled through the ragged V-shaped notch, driving the snow under and through our clothing. We had paused momentarily to drink water and take several pictures before starting down on the Nu River side. It hadn't been until later, when we tried to sneak through a city, that we were arrested and kicked out.

Now we were back in the Nu valley, where we'd been stopped on our first attempt. Could it be that all we had to do was catch the bus? In Hong Kong we had joked about what it would be like to enter the Drung valley after an exhausting journey only to find a big arch across the road announcing "Welcome to Drung Country. Foreigners, please register at the guest house, and feel free to browse at the gift shop just across from McDonald's."

Suddenly it sounded like this was no joke.

Pascal seemed deep in thought. "I am sure he is wrong," he mumbled as he unfolded our topo maps on the rough plank floor. He placed rocks at each corner. "Look." He pointed to the legend at the bottom. "Our map is accurate until 1988 and this man says the road was completed in 1980." The topo showed no roads at all, not even trails, and the Chinese map showed only one thin trail traversing the peaks low, near Gongshan, about ninety miles away in the lower Drung valley. "I think he is wrong," Pascal said again after some time. "All my information indicates that there are no roads entering the Drung valley from Burma or China. I read an article by a Chinese man who entered the lower Drung valley three years ago and he had to use horses and made no mention of roads. But I think the man is right that it is too dangerous to consider crossing the mountains here or higher."

I was too tired to argue about it. "I'm taking a bath," I announced.

"Me too," Sophi said, grabbing her towel and a bar of soap.

We hiked nearly a mile down to the gushing little stream, pursued by a herd of noisy children and a few older villagers. When we reached the bank, Sophi went upstream by the water mills we had passed earlier in the day and then further up to find some seclusion, and I stripped down for my bath. Two women, who had stopped along the path, watched in fascination as I prepared. We had heard that Tibetans traditionally bathe only once a year, so I guess what I was doing was an event. When they realized I was taking off all my clothes, they turned respectfully away, but after I'd put on my swimming suit, they watched me for the entire time.

After swimming and bathing in the icy water, I washed all of my clothes, using a large boulder as a scrub board.

Sophi returned from her bath and washed her clothes too. The creek was beautiful, with its rushing white water, rose quartz, and granite bedrock. We spent a long time washing and relaxing.

When we finally returned, Pascal was very upset. "Where the hell you been all this time?" he bellowed. "I want to wash myself too, you know!"

He calmed down and explained that he had been through a two-hour ordeal. As soon as we'd left, villagers from the surrounding area had made their way to the school to see this strange man and his strange possessions. "They press in on me," he lamented, hugging himself. "I can't cook! I can't write! I can't do anything! And then," he wailed in disgust, "and then, they start spitting!" He spread his arms out dramatically to indicate the floor, which was covered with globs of spittle.

GETTING ENOUGH FOOD to eat in Menkung turned out to be a problem. This area was in a rain shadow, and farming was not nearly as productive as in the previous areas we had traveled through. When we had arrived, we had told the schoolteacher we wanted to purchase chickens, eggs, and bread from the people in order to make our precious stores last longer. He had agreed and promised that in the morning he would have these things. Morning came and no food. Pascal and Sophi waited expectantly, but I finally took matters into my own hands and went "shopping." I soon found that the people here spoke no Chinese and used little money. I hiked until I met a small group of people and acted out a chicken laying an egg, indicating that I wanted to trade money for eggs. The Tibetans laughed and laughed, spoke among themselves, then laughed some more. I could only imagine what they were saying. I laughed with them, then more frantically tried to get my point across. Finally, an old man took one of my yuan notes, held up seven fingers, and disappeared. Twenty minutes later, when he hadn't returned, I figured I had given away a yuan. Just as I was getting up to leave, the man appeared with a hat containing seven small white chicken eggs. An hour later I returned to our room with, besides the eggs, a chicken and four ears of corn. We quickly cooked a meal. Later the schoolteacher came by and offered to take us to the monastery above Menkung. He made no explanation as to why none of the food we had requested had been brought.

Most of the country here was cultivated in corn. As we walked along the fields, we saw people at work, weeding by hand and singing. The monastery itself was small and ancient. As was the custom, we walked once around the building clockwise before entering. Then an old, barefoot monk in dirty red robes came out of the cavelike interior to meet us. Most of his teeth were gone, and he showed us his hands, which were swollen and badly deformed by arthritis. He took both of my hands in his and drew me into the darkness inside. Sitting on a small wood platform covered with furs, which I realized must be his bed at night and his chair by day, he grasped my hands, pulled me beside him, and stared deeply into my eyes. He said several things in Tibetan, then smiled in frustration, gripping my hands even tighter as if he frantically needed to communicate something of infinite importance. Again he looked deeply into my eyes. When he released my hands, he looked tired and even older than before.

Pascal photographed the interior of the monastery. We gave the monk some money and photographs of Tibetan-

Buddhist deities, which he accepted graciously. When we left, we again walked clockwise around the monastery, then back down to the school on the plateau below. On the way, we found someone who had just butchered a cow and purchased several pounds of beef along with a few eggs. As we walked back, I admired the ingenious and intricate system of log conduits used to bring water into the village from the springs high above.

That afternoon I killed and butchered the chicken. All the kids came to help, and with so many pairs of little hands, we had it plucked and dressed in no time. Sophi was able to get mushrooms, so we ate a good meal of mushrooms, chicken, and fresh cucumbers. We had been promised that someone would bring fresh bread, and I was hungry for it, but none arrived. I set out to "shop" for bread and finally found a woman who indicated that I should follow her into the house. I thought she had misunderstood me, because instead of getting bread, she finished cooking a huge meal of hand-pulled barley noodles in soup with onions, potatoes, and meat. Her three sons, husband, father, and (I think) the second wife all gathered around the fire pit, laughing and eating walnuts. They laughed and laughed, and I laughed with them. Her father spoke about as much Chinese as I did, and I managed, with much effort, a simple conversation. The interior of the house was cleaner and more ornate than any of the other Tibetan houses I had been in, with many nice pots and pans and wooden utensils. The husband helped cook the meal. I ate three servings of the delicious soup. I hadn't realized how hungry I was. After the meal, the two women and the husband carefully cooked three loaves of flat corn bread on a large cast-iron pan over the fire. For light they used pine faggots, which sat in a little cast-iron cage hung by a wire from the roof. When the bread was done, the woman packed it in a large pan, and the husband lit me a couple of pine splinters and took me to the door. I was overcome with gratitude for the kindness these people had shown to me, a total stranger. I thanked them in Chinese and pressed a five-yuan note into the woman's hands. She looked at it curiously, then gave it to the younger of her two sons.

ON SUNDAY, SEPTEMBER 19, I rose early and ambled down to the stream to wash my face. When I returned, Pascal and Sophi were already up and dressed, and Pascal told me that they had to go to another village to visit with some official who was the chief of this area. "The people of this village are afraid to help us," Pascal said. "They think they will get into trouble. That is probably why they lied to us about the road. Anyway, I must try and get permission for us to travel south because I want horses and porters and someone to guide us into the lower Drung valley."

"Pascal!" I started.

He jumped in and cut me off. "I know. You want a big adventure, but I have to think of safety first. The mountains are too high—I think it is too dangerous—that is my decision!"

"Let's just try," I begged, "if not by the north, then at least let's cross here. If it is too difficult, we can always come back, get more food, and then go downstream."

"No!" Pascal said loudly, almost shouting. Then his eyes softened and his voice lowered. "Wade, it is not for me. Sophi is not well and though she tries to be strong, she is really very afraid of the mountains. We must consider her in our decisions."

This stopped me. I couldn't imagine Sophi being afraid of anything, but since they were always gabbing away in French, I decided Pascal knew better than I what was going on with her.

I decided to stay back and write in my journal because I disliked dealing with public officials and wouldn't be of any use anyway: all the discussion would be in French and Chinese.

It had been exactly one month since my arrival in Hong Kong, but with all the experiences we'd had, it seemed much longer. I spent the day by myself, wandering high in the mountains above the Nu River. After swimming in the ice-cold glacier-fed waters of the torrent, I napped in the sun on a smooth, black, water-polished boulder, then went out "begging" for food.

Money was just about useless here, as these people traded directly for clothes, pots and pans, and other necessities. Right now the most valuable trade item seemed to be mushrooms. I had seen mule caravan after caravan loaded down with barrels of salted mushrooms or leather bags of dried mushrooms. They were delicious. Pascal thought there was also trade with tiger, snow leopard, and wolf skins, some medicinal plants found only here, and the musk of animals, although we hadn't seen any of it.

People had been bringing us food, but it was the wrong kind. We had enough walnuts and cucumbers for two months, but getting eggs, meat, potatoes, butter, and salt seemed to be about impossible. There was a lot of fruit here, and although most of it was small, we were given pomegranates, pears, and apples, along with many little peaches. Clothing and belongings were also scarce and varied, and I saw people in both Chinese clothes and traditional Tibetan wools and skins. For amulets, many wore Buddhist beads and had pictures of the Dalai Lama and the Panchen Lama, while at the same time others wore Communist stars, badges, and pins, as well as pictures of Mao Tse-tung engraved on brass pennants. Pascal believed that the majority of these people were better off as a result of China's takeover and that they knew it. Still, there was little surplus, and from what I had read about China's bloody occupation, I couldn't understand how any of them could be the least bit patriotic toward China. Clearly this issue was more complex than it first appeared.

Pascal and Sophi staggered in at dusk, looking like survivors of the Long March. It had taken them over six hours to cross through the desert of the Nu River valley. They had carried no water, and the Tibetan public official had not offered them any food, so they had gone the entire day without eating. I mixed electrolyte-replacement drinks from my first-aid kit and gave them each half a Power Bar. I finally asked Pascal about the interview. He smiled weakly and said, "I got authorization for us to cross the mountains here and the villagers have promised to help us." I couldn't believe it! I let out a war whoop and hugged Pascal as hard as I could. This meant we would cross the mountains between the Irrawaddy and Nu Rivers through a 15,000-foot pass and between two 21,000-foot mountains, eventually arriving in the upper Irrawaddy valley. Granted, we would not be traveling quite from the headwaters, but we would still travel through the very wild country of the upper Irrawaddy valley to where it became known as the Drung River.

At first I was elated. But, as the evening wore on, I started feeling uneasy. Something wasn't right. During dinner Sophi and Pascal were strangely quiet and avoided my eyes. "O.K., what haven't you told me?" I finally demanded.

"You won't like this," he started, then paused. "You see, there is a very small military outpost in Ridong. They patrol this part of the Burmese border. I am taking us there. Most likely they will all be Tibetans and will be surprised to see us and will want to help us. We would have to get permission from them anyway to go down the Irrawaddy River because it is on the Burmese border."

"Why?" I demanded incredulously. "Since when did we start *having* to get permission?"

"This is different," he huffed. "This is the border. We must do things as legally as possible."

FIVE

Lion's Den

PASCAL AND SOPHI had pushed hard physically, so I was surprised to find that Sophi was not in her sleeping bag when I awoke early the next morning. Pascal snored peacefully away as I gingerly unzipped the screen door and buckled on my sandals. Scrambled eggs and pork fat lay already cooked in a covered pan on warm coals. Outside it was a beautiful sunny morning, although thunderclouds were building in the west. By afternoon it would be raining again. Standing at the gate to the school courtyard, I saw her. Sitting on a boulder at the edge of the alluvial platform on which Menkung is built, she stared out across the twisting canyons of the Nu River, with its churning chocolate water, toward the distant snowcapped peaks of the sacred mountain Kar-Kar-Po thirty miles south. She turned and smiled as I approached, her skin golden and her face radiant in the early-morning light. We sat together for a little while enjoying the beautiful scene in silence.

"I was just thinking," I started. "Do you remember how excited we were in Hong Kong about this trip?"

"Oh Wade, you get excited about everything. But yes, I think I know what you're talking about. This certainly isn't the way I expected it to be either. I'm not sure anymore what Pascal is thinking, or what he's trying to do. Sometimes his excuses for changing plans don't make sense to me, and I feel like he is holding something back. When I translate for him he often lies. Sometimes even I don't know if what I'm saying is true, and that bothers me. This morning I was thinking again about Tiananmen Square."

I had read the newspaper articles. She had been a student there at the time and I asked her to tell me about it. She smiled.

"It started out as a really happy thing. In the beginning there wasn't much of a political issue. The students were voicing their opinions aloud, and it was the first time anyone had been able to do that and get away with it. There was excitement in the streets, we could all feel it. The students were so excited and were tasting freedom for the first time. The actual demonstrations, which came later, were a result of this excitement, and again, in the early stages, it wasn't political at all. They wanted better conditions for study, more freedom to go abroad, and easier access to higher education. Of course the government didn't like it, but you have to understand that the government itself was split into two factions and couldn't figure out what to do.

"But then things began to change. Agitators came from the country and stirred things up. These were bad people, troublemakers, and they started pushing the movement in new directions. Things became more political as the students and others involved in the demonstrations began shouting demands to have democracy and to get rid of the old government. It started getting ugly. Some of the politicians were sympathetic to the cause of the students, and one even visited Tiananmen Square and spoke to the students. He disappeared immediately, of course, and has not been heard of since, as far as I know. He 'went to the country for a rest,' as we say in China. It was one of the earliest indications of how serious things were getting.

"Every night we watched TV and listened to the radio. Two announcers who were partial to the cause of the students kept us up to date about the events. One evening they came on and announced that they had both been fired. Things got darker and uglier as the weeks went on. I couldn't go to Tiananmen Square myself because the students didn't allow foreigners to participate in their demonstrations, but many of us were as active as we could be in other ways.

"The students were incredibly well organized—too well, many people thought then. There is a strongly held belief that the leadership came from the outside, that the students themselves couldn't possibly have structured the movement in such a way. I don't know.

"We started hearing on the radio that massive forces were being moved into Tiananmen, that the army was coming, although we didn't know which army or from where. Each night I would see truckloads of exhausted students returning from Tiananmen and truckloads of fresh students all fired up, shaking their fists and yelling slogans as they were being driven back out to the Square. Some of the students stayed day and night, refusing to eat or sleep.

"The news continued to say that the military was coming, and I remember when they first began to arrive. We all went out into the street and stopped the trucks coming in. Most of the soldiers were very young, and they had been carefully shielded from what was going on and knew nothing. We pleaded with them to go back. 'Please, please don't come and kill us at Tiananmen,' we begged. They were shocked, and most of them returned. The Chinese army is called the People's Army because it is separate from the government, or maybe you could say it is a government itself, and many of the military leaders refused to move their troops on the students. I heard that some of these leaders disappeared also. In the end, it wasn't the military who moved in, it was a special division of the police force.

"One evening Li Peng made a special broadcast on the radio. It was terrible. He recounted many tragedies in Chinese history and talked about how there were bad things happening now. He said there were influences—meaning the students—threatening to tear apart the country, and that something was going to be done. Oh, it was so awful to hear him talk! We knew something horrible was going to happen, but we weren't sure what. Within a week after this—well, you know the rest. No one knows for sure how many people died. I don't know if the government even made a count. Officially the incident didn't occur, and I am sure everyone on both sides of the issue wishes it hadn't. Within a month we were all shipped back to our countries on commercial airlines and on special flights. You know, nobody expected things to turn out the way they did, in the beginning. It started out as more of an adventure. But I can remember feeling uneasy, long before things got horrible. I feel like that right now."

We sat in silence for a few minutes. I looked over at her and saw tears brimming in her eyes. I didn't know what to say.

"I cooked some eggs and pork fat for breakfast," she said at last. "Maybe we should go heat it up."

She stood suddenly, and I caught her arm.

"No, Wade. I'm O.K., really."

Turning quickly, she walked back toward the school. A little later I rose and followed her.

THE NEXT MORNING Sophi and Pascal had a long talk. Pascal told me about their discussion. "Sophi has been really disappointed in the lack of adventure we have experienced so far, Wade. You know, I told her about the last trip, how we got arrested three times, how we hid in the back of trucks, how we got up at four in the morning to sneak through towns, how we were rained on and snowed on. I told her everything so she would understand what we would be up for and would make the decision to come based on these things. But this trip has gone so smoothly so far. We expected it to be much more difficult. You did and I did, and we built Sophi up to expect it to be a real adventure, and it just hasn't happened yet, even though we have had some great experiences. It hasn't been that challenging, and she is starting to lose her enthusiasm. She thinks I am too reserved and careful."

Pascal and I talked for quite a while, and I told him how frustrated I too had also been when he started changing our plans. He *was* too reserved and careful, I said, and I didn't have much control over the situation when he decided to change things around. Again we talked about the incident of crossing the Nu Mountains two years before. I reminded him how I'd had to practically drag him through the mountains and how we'd been fine until we tried to sneak through a city. We talked for a few more minutes, then Pascal left to look for more food. I felt better. It was a difficult conversation, but a good one. I could tell it had been hard for Pascal to hear the same complaints twice in the same day from two different people.

• • •

OUR FOOD PROBLEM was getting serious. We hadn't been able to obtain enough food to eat each day and were slowly using up our precious supplies meant for the climb. Sophi and I finally confronted the schoolteacher about the supplies he had promised but not delivered. "You just don't understand," he told us, and Sophi translated for me. "You're used to being able to buy what you want, but here there isn't that much extra of anything. When you get some eggs from a family in the morning, those are eggs that the family was going to eat that day. It's the same with everything. You are going to Ridong in a few days and there's nothing there. The people eat only meat and almost no vegetables. You probably won't be able to use your money at all." He went on for a long time, and was truly upset. We apologized to him, asking him to forgive our ignorance.

In the past two days, I had become slightly acquainted with a man who lived half a mile from the village. Filthy beyond description in his crusted homespun, he followed me around shouting questions and demanding responses in poor Chinese. One evening as I was walking up to Menkung, he suddenly appeared on the trail. Barring the path, he offered to sell me corn flour at a ridiculously high price, about sixty cents a pound. I decided to go ahead and buy from him because we needed it badly, so I followed him back to his house. As I walked into the building, I was shocked at what I found. The place was appallingly filthy and the stench was almost unbearable. An incredible clutter lay strewn about. The rough plank floor had a thick layer of dirt, mud, and manure, as well as rotting rags and food lying on it, and the fireplace was littered with rotting food and bowls of partially consumed chang. The man shakily poured me some chang into an unwashed bowl, then hurriedly left the room to fetch the corn flour. As my eyes adjusted to the dark interior, I realized that a dirty pile of rags in the far corner of the room was covering up a person. I went to inspect and found an old, white-haired lady suffering from severe dysentery. Blood and feces soaked the lower part of her bed and the stench was now more than I could stand. Beneath the ragged blanket, insects that looked like weevils scurried to hide themselves further within the folds as I pulled back the covers. I could tell the woman had been there for a long time, and she didn't look as though she was getting better. The man entered the room with a sack of flour, and the look of pain and hopelessness on his face when he saw me examining his mother was worse than I had seen before.

He had little flour, and I bought it all at his high price, realizing he desperately needed money to buy medicine. I left with much to think about on my walk back to the village. It had been so easy for me to pass judgment on the man's character without knowing what he was about. I realized now that all the time I'd thought he was hounding me, he'd been trying to communicate the need for medicine for his sick mother.

The next day I went back to the man's house. We desperately needed more food, and by now the other villagers were almost entirely unwilling to sell any to me. I thought perhaps I could buy his flour, and give him more money for his sick mother. The children took me to the top floor, where I found him passed out by a bucket of chang. He was so drunk he could not stand or walk without my help. I half-dragged him into a small storeroom on the second floor of the house, where we found two sacks, one holding about six pounds of corn flour, the other about ten pounds of barley flour. I asked him if he would sell it all to me and he said yes, but in his drunken state he had no idea what amount of money he wanted. Between his being drunk and both of us being able to speak only marginal Chinese, the conversation became extremely tedious. Five young children stared on in apprehension as they watched me try to trade what must have seemed to them a few scraps of paper for what was probably all the food in the house. I pressed forty yuan into the man's shaking hand and asked him if that was enough. Without looking at it he said it was fine. I hoisted the two sacks off the floor and started to leave. A frail boy about four or five lunged forward and threw his arms around the sacks of flour, his weight pulling them back to the floor. He was completely naked, and his little ribs showed through his thin brown skin. The commotion roused the man from his drunken stupor. He stood awkwardly, and angrily admonished the young child. He yelled again and swatted at the little boy until he released the bag he held. I tried to offer the flour back to the man. The child again lunged for the sacks, but the man caught the boy and held him back, motioning angrily for me to leave. Again I hoisted the flour onto my back and then slowly climbed down the notched ladder to the barnyard below. The little boy began to cry, and as I walked away from the house, I could hear him wailing. I sat down by the trail and tried to decide if I should take the flour back. We were leaving early the next morning and it would be impossible to find more by then. Also, I had given the man a lot of money, probably four or five times what the flour was worth. Surely he could use some of it to trade for food the next day. But I didn't know this for sure, and as I walked back to the school, I couldn't shake off the feeling that I had done something terrible.

ALL OUR PREPARATIONS were complete, so that evening Pascal and Sophi drank corn liquor—or *jiu*, as it was called—with the schoolteacher and a few other men, and said their final good-byes, while I went out. Someone had started playing a Chinese fiddle in the court outside our door, and a large circle of people started dancing and singing. I joined the dancers. At first everyone laughed and jeered, but after a time they settled down and seemed to forget I was there. I sang the simple melodies and danced the Tibetan dances I had learned in Bitu. I had grown tired of being a constant source of bewilderment and entertainment for the people. I knew I could never be Tibetan, but for a few minutes, I just wanted to belong, to be part of a large group of people, not some strange alien whose every action and every possession contrasted so sharply with his surroundings that anyone who saw him stopped to stare. In the deep darkness of the courtyard as I danced around a small pear tree holding hands with fifty other people, no one paid any special attention to me. I yearned to just belong. For a few moments, I felt as though I did.

WE GOT UP early on September 22 to pack our things. According to previous arrangements, two men arrived with three horses and a mule. The schoolchildren were let out to see us off. All the older villagers within several miles also showed up. Soon after we left, it began to rain. We climbed steadily for several hours through dense forest, occasionally passing great fir trees, some larger than two yards across at the base.

The rain continued, and we finally stopped for lunch, taking refuge beneath a huge "widowmaker" branch hung up in the lower part of one of the pines. Everything was soaked, and I figured it would take hours to get a decent fire going. The two Tibetans, who had much more experience than we did at making fires from wet material, had a few tricks I'd never seen before. Splitting a dead tree, they chopped out dry wood from the center with their ax. Next, one of them produced a block of pitch wood, used for lanterns and to start fires, and cut several splinters. He lit those splinters, then piled on wet wood while the second man took out a simple bellows made of the skin from the leg of a yak sewn tightly around a wooden pipe. He pumped it like an accordion, and within fifteen minutes we had a roaring blaze. After some rest, we got in another good hour of hiking before the rain forced us to stop again.

It rained hard all night, but Pascal's tiny mountaineering tent was comfortable and dry. Sophi had a cold and coughed continually, but at least we were warm.

The next day we hiked through the dense fir forest. By noon it had quit raining, and when we stopped for lunch, the sun even came out for a while. Strands of green moss hung from the branches of the firs. The place was a mushroom paradise; I had never seen so many different kinds. Our Tibetan guides feasted on them raw, and I envied their knowledge of which ones were edible.

Eventually the clouds cleared away to reveal new snow on the peaks around us. We crossed through a 12,000-foot pass, dropped 5,000 feet into a U-shaped valley, and then climbed up again to about 12,000 feet, near the tree line, and camped for the night. Sophi still wasn't feeling well, so she rode one of the horses the last few miles.

I didn't feel so well myself and went to bed early. Sometime in the middle of the night I heard the sound of retching. I switched on my head lamp and found Pascal on his hands and knees. The bottom of Sophi's and my sleeping bags were soaked in vomit. "So sorry, so sorry," Pascal kept saying between retches. We cleaned up the best we could and went back to bed, but I was drained both physically and emotionally. It seemed that the only clean, dry environment we'd had was now violated.

IT SNOWED ON us most of the way the next day, and the horses became increasingly uncooperative. Cold, wet, and sick, we trudged on. At 15,000 feet there were still yaks grazing on the sparse clumps of grass. Gasping for air, I watched our two Tibetan packers pause at the top of the pass for a moment to light up cigarettes before continuing down the other side.

We descended until we hit tree line again, and the snow turned to rain. Finally we stopped to cook lunch. Pascal was too sick to eat, but I heated milk and he managed to force down a few mouthfuls of soggy bread-and-butter tea. I, too, was getting sicker. Sophi coughed continually, as she had been doing the past four days. The two Tibetans quickly repacked the four animals and threw wood on the fire so if another traveler came along in the next few hours, he wouldn't have the trouble of starting a fire from scratch, a monumental task in this weather.

We traveled on through the rain, pushing hard because we wanted to reach Ridong before dark. Finally we arrived at the first fork of the Irrawaddy River. It was small, hardly more than a stream. I found it hard to imagine that this became the main river of Burma, but of course we were somewhere near the headwaters. We turned upstream, and after a while started passing people and houses built of logs with roofs made of long, split shakes. The people, who were out in their fields harvesting barley, stopped their work and regarded us suspiciously. As we neared the first of five small villages, we were assailed by a pack of dogs. Quickly I pulled my ice ax off one of the packsaddles, and we managed to drive them back with rocks. Several times we stopped so the packers could ask people if they would be willing to put us up for the night, but each time the answer was no. I was amazed at how many of the people had eye infections. Later I learned that because of the extreme cold in winter, there are no chimneys here, so people's eyes are constantly irritated by the smoke.

Failing to find a place for the night, we decided to proceed directly to the small Chinese military base. Pascal insisted that if the two Tibetans would vouch that we had verbal authorization to come to Ridong, and if we just walked right in as though we belonged there, the military would go along. I hated the idea. We were walking into a lion's den.

As we neared the camp, it seemed even more stupid. Worse, our two Tibetan packers, while still good-natured, were becoming progressively more bossy as the day wore on. It got to the point that they were telling us when and where to eat, rest, even go to the bathroom, and I was getting tired of it. Then they decided that the one who could speak Chinese would take Sophi and Pascal ahead to meet the military captain while the other and I stayed back with the horses. Eventually, I got tired of waiting, but when I started to follow in their footsteps, the packer decided he wanted me to ride the lead mule while he led it. I guess this was for prestige in some way, but we almost got into a fist-fight over the issue. I usually refuse to ride horses or mules. Years ago I became deeply prejudiced against cowboys, or anything associated with them, after many unpleasant encounters in my native Idaho. But this man was stubborn and refused to let me pass until I finally gave in and mounted up. When we passed through the next little clump of houses, all the people stopped and stared. The packer puffed out his chest and strutted along leading the mule, and I felt like a bigger ass than the one I was riding!

The military base consisted of four small whitewashed adobe buildings arranged in a square, all in various degrees of disrepair. In the middle of the buildings a broken basketball hoop stood in a small flooded exercise yard. Pigs, chickens, and dogs roamed freely about, and the tin on the roofs of the buildings was peeling off in many places. The soldiers who came out to meet us were clean, but casually dressed, wearing a mixture of army and civilian clothes. They wore sneakers, and all of them looked very young. I found out in later conversation that the oldest was twenty-six and most around eighteen, with some even as young as seventeen. Half were Tibetans, and the other half, Chinese.

I was led to a small cubicle that contained the only TV for perhaps fifty or a hundred square miles. A small satellite dish mounted in the exercise yard looked about as alien there as our tent had on the roof of a Tibetan house, and a row of rough wooden benches in front of the house with a chalkboard nailed up on the outside wall constituted the base "meeting hall."

Inside I found Sophi and Pascal in deep discussion with

the man we called the captain, though we didn't really know his rank. He was a short Chinese man about twenty-five years old with a bulldog jaw and a surly manner. He questioned Sophi and Pascal at length and made out a detailed report. As before, Pascal told the man our trip was, of course, perfectly legitimate, that the authorities up until now had been very helpful, and that he hoped the military would also be able to supply us with some assistance on this difficult journey. When Pascal explained what we wanted to do, the captain took out and unfolded a little dirty road map and indicated that there was no trail to the Irrawaddy valley from here (indeed, he didn't know for sure who the Drung people were anyway). He told us we couldn't get there from here.

The conversation dragged on and on, and as usual, Pascal and Sophi talked in French, freezing me out. Then one of the men, Dr. Liu, the second in command, took me to the infirmary to meet a second physician, Dr. Yu, a kindly man several years younger than I was. On one side of the room was a cabinet full of medicine, a stethoscope, and a few acupuncture needles. There were no injectable drugs. As we poached eggs over a small woodstove, I visited with him the best I could with my limited Chinese. Much later the captain brought Pascal in for the doctors to examine. They gave him some pills. Next someone brought in an older Tibetan man who was introduced to us as the chief of Ridong, and he invited us to sleep in his house for the night.

We had walked only about fifty yards toward the chief's house when a young soldier came running after us and told us we had to wait for the captain. The rain was pouring down and our packs were heavy. We had hiked more than twelve hours straight over a 15,000-foot pass, and all three of us were sick. For twenty minutes we stood in the rain cursing and complaining until finally the captain arrived carrying an iron rod as a walking stick. He briskly escorted us on the half-hour walk to the chief's house.

There were only three rough board beds in the house, so the family made up other beds on the floor. Then the chief, his wife, his brother-in-law, and his two children packed up their blankets and moved to a neighbor's house half a mile away for the night. Later the chief came back and prepared a meal of rice and fried potatoes, although Pascal couldn't eat at all and I could eat only a little.

The chief spoke simple Chinese and told us many things about this area. We knew from Pascal's research that agriculture was hard here, and little more than an uncertain crop of barley could be grown in the short three-month growing season. The man said that now the Chinese government provided a ration of rice for each family, and this had greatly reduced the uncertainty of year-to-year life that had traditionally been the case here. They were also freely provided with clothes, we were told, but judging from how ragged and patched everyone's apparel looked, it must have been a long time since the last shipment.

We talked until late in the evening, then finally the captain of the military base, the village chief, and a few other men who had materialized mercifully left and we went to bed. I didn't sleep well at all but became increasingly sicker. We had eaten a lot of the rancid raw pork fat the Tibetan packers carried in great supply when they traveled, and I felt maybe that was what had gotten me.

WE KNEW WE were in Ridong and that Ridong was at one of the forks of the upper Irrawaddy River, but we didn't know exactly which fork or how far up. After studying our contour maps and the country around us, I came up with two possibilities. One put us twenty miles from the upper Drung valley, and the other put us about forty. Pascal, of course, was certain it was the farthest distance and said if there wasn't a trail, he didn't know how we could possibly attempt to follow the Irrawaddy down. Pascal said he doubted we could make it, and the chief of the village said he couldn't provide a guide.

I finally came unglued. I was sick and tired of Pascal's pessimism and reservations about everything. Even though having horses and people who knew how to get from one place to the next had cut our travel time to half of what we had expected, it had cut out a lot of the adventure and free-dom he'd promised. I was fed up with letting someone else decide where we were camping, what we were eating, and when we were resting, and I was tired of Pascal getting cold feet every time we got into a situation in which we might have to take a chance and rely totally on ourselves for a change!

"Why in the heck did you invite me along?" I said. "Why have me purchase climbing equipment and dehy-drated food, and cart them all the way across Tibet if you weren't even going to go somewhere we could use them? If you aren't willing to go down the Irrawaddy, I will take my third of the food and go by myself! I won't feel badly about leaving you because I know you will never stick your head out far enough to need me, and anyway it is you who is not keeping up your part of the deal. I'll just be finishing our original plan!"

We were still arguing when our Tibetan porters (I had no idea where they had spent the night) ducked through the doorway and stiffly asked for their wages. Pascal doled out the promised three hundred yuan, a significant sum of money here. I saw the chief's eyes grow large as Sophi recounted the bills and gave the money to them. They informed us there was no known road to the Drung valley from here and offered to take us back to Menkung with them. When Sophi translated this, I shouted, "I will go to *hell* before going back to Menkung!" They then offered to gather more information and attempt to take us through the mountains to the Drung valley. "No! I'm not going with them," I insisted, "and I'm not giving any more responsibility to someone else to solve our problems!" When Sophi translated this, they left.

WE WENT BACK to the military base to try to figure out where we were in relation to the Irrawaddy River. As we were discussing this, the captain appeared and promptly marched Sophi and Pascal into his office for a conference. "Bad news," Sophi said when I checked with them an hour later. "The captain has decided to prepare a room for us on the base, and we are being placed under supervision until arrangements can be made to leave for the Drung valley."

"You mean we are under arrest?" I said.

"Not technically, but something like that," she replied. We were escorted back to the village to collect our things, then sent to a small room that had only two plank board beds. After a complicated discussion, Sophi negotiated our getting one more bed and yak-hair rugs to pad the boards.

It was a horrible night. My guts were already sore from the dysentery, and the food poisoning gave me unbearable cramps. At least once an hour I had to get up, trundle out the door, and find a place in the field. There were no latrines here and no running water of any kind. Finally in the morning the cramps let up and I slept a little. Later one of the soldiers brought us some steamed bread and rice soup, which I ate a little of, and I began to feel better. Dr. Yu came in to check on me and gave me some medicine.

After a while the village chief came by to negotiate porters for our trip downriver. Pascal wanted to hire enough porters to carry everything so he would be free to walk and take pictures. He also wanted to take a large reserve of food so we could stay some time in the upper Drung valley without being too much of a burden on the people there.

There were several problems with this. First of all, the chief told us these people were right in the middle of harvest, and anyone who might be strong enough to pack our things would be busy. He said we would have to offer a great deal of money to get anyone to take seven or eight days off to go with us. Second, we couldn't get any accurate information about the route and were still not certain exactly where on the Irrawaddy we were. The chief told us he had located two old men who had allegedly made the trip to the Drung valley. One had gone only once, when he was a young boy, and at that time there was a reasonably good trail, he said. They had made the trip in three and a half hard days. The second man had made the trip in 1979. He said it had taken them five days one way and that the trail was very bad; it had been all but obliterated by the rain forest. They had had to build bridges and repair parts of the trail just to get by on foot. Maybe he was exaggerating, but it didn't matter. His report was enough to discourage the village men and, of course, Pascal. The chief made three trips to and from the village, each time returning to say that it didn't look good.

I was the third problem. I didn't like the idea of using

porters. It was against my basic nature. I'd much rather carry a large load and rely on myself, even though I reluctantly agreed with Pascal that extra food would be a good insurance policy. Also, these people were not like Sherpas, the elite Tibetan trekkers who have been assisting Himalayan mountain-climbing expeditions for decades. They were not used to this kind of work, as we were the first foreigners to come here and try to hire them. And although I was confident that with ropes and climbing techniques we could get through difficult terrain, how would the porters get back by themselves to their village after we reached the Drung valley?

THAT EVENING WE visited for several hours with the captain and a few other men. The captain broke out a small private stock of sugar, proudly announcing that it was the only sugar to be found in the valley. We sat around a woodstove in his quarters, drank tea sweetened with his sugar, and talked about the differences between America, France, and China.

The captain proudly told us Ridong was the second most difficult military base to serve at in China. The winters were brutally cold, and supplies, mail, and even food were limited, as everything had to be brought in by horseback. The only generator for the camp was broken down at present, or so we were told, and there was no way for them to transmit by radio. This left the captain with absolute power over what to do with us, and I felt he quite liked it that way. So far he appeared more than willing to help, and it didn't seem as though he was going to interfere with our plans to go downriver. It could change in a heartbeat, though, especially if there was contact with higher authority.

It continued raining for two more days. I was finally getting over my case of dysentery, and the food poisoning had run its course. Feeling stronger and more energetic from two nights in a row of good sleep, I arose early and decided to take a hike up the Irrawaddy. The people of Ridong and the surrounding villages were up with the first light. Using small hand sickles, they were frantically trying to harvest the barley crop before it rotted in the field. They tied it up in clumps, then carried it up to the top rooms of the houses to be dried by the smoke of the cooking fires. Later, once the monsoon ended, they would thresh the barley outside using whip-sticks.

As I climbed, the valley became steep, with vertical limestone walls. The headwaters of the Irrawaddy cascaded through great blocks of limestone and plummeted over high cliffs. In other places it formed still, deep-green pools, which seemed to invite you to dive in from the cliffs above—in more congenial weather.

I had been told that the yak herd was high on the plateau above, and I decided to try and reach it and then get back by that evening. The trail wound its way up the steep canyon, occasionally crossing the river on rickety cantilever bridges. I climbed high into some beautiful alpine meadows where thousands of prayer flags, laboriously planted on bamboo poles, stretched off into the distance as far as I could see.

It continued to pour, and soon I was soaked to the skin. At the edge of the meadow I met three Tibetan brothers, the oldest of whom could speak Chinese. I eventually convinced one of them to sell me his machetelike bush knife with its wooden sheath. Pascal and I had agreed earlier that we would need one in the rain forest of the lower Irrawaddy River.

The four of us took refuge in a small, deserted log cabin and built a roaring blaze in the fire pit. The boys knew of Pascal, Sophi, and me. They said that word of the three strange foreigners who wanted to follow the old slave road to the lower Irrawaddy had already reached the upper camps. Slave road? I had not heard of it before. Could this be connected to the Drung, I wondered? They told me the yak herd was still six hours away, and although it was already late afternoon I set off again and went for several more hours before turning back. I regretted not telling Pascal and Sophi I might spend the night—otherwise I would have continued on.

On my return I was stopped by an old farmer, who invited me to eat with his family. This was the family that the three boys I had met earlier belonged to, although I didn't learn this until several days later. In the dim firelight the man's daughter practiced writing Chinese characters using a small burned stick as a charcoal pencil. I gave her one of my two good Cross pens and a refill. Now I had to keep track of my remaining pen. But to see her face light up with joy was well worth the sacrifice.

PASCAL AND SOPHI were not in our rooms when I got back. I found them in the rear of a small storage room gambling with five of the soldiers. Two bottles of jiu were nearly empty, and a third bottle held a burning candle that cast eerie shadows on seven gray, intent faces.

"The captain was looking for you," Sophi said, as she slapped her hand down.

"Since when did he decide to be my mother," I shot back irritably.

"I think we need to have a discussion," Pascal said, rising from the table and folding the thick wad of bills he had won into his pocket.

Back in our room we evaluated the present situation. Trying to negotiate for porters was proving to be a tedious and dubious task. Worse, the captain was starting to act strangely. The day before, Pascal had gone on a "hunting" trip in spite of the rain, and the captain had panicked when he discovered that Pascal had left without his permission. He had sent a soldier to bring him back. I had laughed to myself at the time, knowing most likely Pascal would see the soldier first and evade him; he had, arriving back at camp hours before the poor, distraught private. The captain had then begun to question us extensively about our backgrounds and about the things we had already told him. He was particularly interested in Pascal's mythical grandfather. Unlike his missionary grandfather, Pascal's new explorer grandfather was based on a French adventurer he had read about in a book, so he was able to tell a very believable story. Still, the sudden inquisition troubled us. We agreed to leave in two days for the lower Irrawaddy, porters or no porters. We also decided to give up any thoughts we'd entertained of traveling to the headwaters of the Irrawaddy, which was heartbreaking for Sophi and me. We felt we could leave Ridong without too many problems, but we had no idea how long this situation would remain favorable. We also didn't know when replacement parts for the broken generator would arrive, giving the captain the ability to transmit and receive radio messages.

That night the village chief met with us in the base headquarters, and of course the young military captain sat in on the conversation. We were again told it would be impossible to hire porters, that no one would agree to follow us into the upper Drung valley. He repeated the story about the last man to travel the trail, fifteen years ago, who had spent five and a half harrowing days traversing treacherous cliffs and building bridges over the river.

I thought the man's description sounded like it would be exciting. Not Pascal though. He was all the more certain that we needed porters to carry extra food. Sophi told the two men we were seriously considering going by ourselves without porters. At this the military captain jumped in with his shrill voice and announced he was taking charge of the situation. "Oh God," Pascal groaned. The captain pompously proclaimed his authority was above that of the village chief, and that he personally was going to arrange for us to have seven porters from the village for the trip in two days, and he guaranteed it.

I wasn't sure who was more surprised, the village chief or us. We all stared at the captain in disbelief as he went on to explain that he, himself, was planning to write a book about his experiences while serving in Tibet and that the story of Pascal and his grandfather would add an exciting chapter. He wanted to see us succeed personally as well as professionally, since he believed it was his job to assist foreign friends in this remote place. He then meticulously set out the conditions of our deal, saying what he believed would be the fairest for both parties. He let the village chief have some input, but mostly he called the shots.

Each man would receive seventy yuan a day for his services. To ensure that we made payment, the money would be left with him until the men returned from their trek. Because it had been said that fifteen years ago it took five days for the trip, he reasoned it would take at least six now, so he wanted us to pay up front six days wages for each man.

The whole deal stunk, and I said so to Pascal. I didn't want the villagers to help us against their will. If this trail actually turned out to be bad, I wanted people to take the risk by their own choice for whatever we paid them. Besides, leaving the money with the captain sounded crazy. If the porters freaked out and decided not to cooperate somewhere along the way, we would have to come back here to straighten things out, leaving our food and equipment in the rain forest. Also, we would have no way to be certain that all or any of the money would actually get to the villagers. It was a lot of money for one Chinese person, and although Pascal insisted he trusted the man's integrity, this situation was enough to tempt a saint.

"I don't care!" Pascal shouted. "I don't care about these things! I just want to go to the Drung valley!" He pointed emphatically south with both hands, gesticulating wildly. "If we can't agree among ourselves, we won't get any deal!"

WHEN THE CAPTAIN had told us we would have to stay in Ridong, he had promised we would be fed three meals a day, and we were, although the portions were extremely small. Breakfast at 8:30 consisted of two small pieces of steamed bread each and a bowl of watery rice soup to be shared between the three of us. Lunch at 11:30 was usually a little plate of fried radishes and potatoes shared by the three of us, about three mouthfuls each, and a large bowl of rice. Dinner at 6:30 was the same as lunch, only smaller portions or without the rice. Occasionally I saw the cook, a seventeen-year-old Tibetan from Lhasa, open a can of meat, but except for that first night, we found no meat in our food. We finally managed to purchase fifteen pounds of potatoes from a villager, and Sophi and I cooked up a plate or two of these between meals. We still had ten days' worth of food, but we were trying to keep all of it for our final push into the Drung valley.

The day I returned from my hike up the Irrawaddy, I was shocked to see a caravan of nine pack mules loaded down with large green steel canisters. Apparently the base supplies had arrived. Nearly all the men hurried around, popping open the watertight lids and hauling out bags of rice, cartons of noodles, and large tin cans of meat. I wondered if the parts for the broken generator were also packed somewhere in the menagerie. I caught sight of Pascal surreptitiously recording the event with his Nikon from the door of our room. It was so like him to walk a razor's edge with the authorities. We had been specifically told not to photograph anything or anyone on the base.

Later in the evening we were called into the office, the captain's bedroom, and introduced to a man we had never met before. It was obvious that this new man was the higher authority because the captain didn't say a word during the entire conversation, something I never would have believed. I decided to call the new captain "Captain Big" to distinguish him from the original captain. This also gave me an excuse to refer to the other captain as "Captain Little," which pleased me, because I was growing distinctly less fond of the guy with each passing hour. Captain Big interviewed us carefully, then told us that, as far as he could tell, our situation was being handled appropriately, and that he would allow things to continue as they had. He apologized for the meager food rations and explained that there just wasn't that much available. They were only supplied every two months and had to make things last the best they could until the next caravan arrived. Sophi assured him we greatly appreciated what food we received and also asked to buy a few pounds of rice. He said he would check and see if there was enough, but that it should be possible.

THE OTHER SHOE dropped the next day. The village chief came to our room along with Captain Little and two young Tibetan men. One of the men was introduced to us, and it was explained that he would be the leader of the porters. He spoke simple Chinese and proudly announced he would be ready to leave in four days. "Four days!" Pascal shouted. "You promised we would leave tomorrow!" Captain Little seemed unruffled as he explained that it was snowing up high where the yaks were being kept and the man had to go up and bring the animals down; otherwise one might die. "We pay a lot of money because now it is an inconvenience for you. You can take some of the money and hire someone to bring down your yaks," Pascal reasoned, although with his wild gesticulations and red face, he looked anything but reasonable. Sophi translated this and the villager replied.

"It isn't possible for someone to bring down our yaks. Only we know our animals' names and the yaks will not obey anyone other than their owners. For us, there is nothing more important than these animals. Even the barley of our fields and the rice from the government is uncertain. Some winters our yaks are the only source of food."

"Then we will leave by ourselves!" Pascal decided with finality.

After Sophi translated this, there was a long pause, and the chief of the village and Captain Little looked knowingly at each other, as though this was a possibility they had already discussed. Finally Captain Little spoke, and his careful articulation of the sentences indicated to me that he had rehearsed in his mind what he was going to say.

"This village has a council that decides everything. This council is under a larger council that is under the government of the autonomous region of Xizang. This council has decided, and I the military captain substantiate the decision, that for your own safety, you will not be permitted to leave Ridong for the Drung valley without the porters."

"Then we will return to Menkung and try from there," Pascal ventured, and again Captain Little replied.

"That also will not be permitted without the approval of the council."

"So, let's meet this council now and get this thing straightened out," Pascal demanded angrily.

"I am sorry. The head of the council is in the mountains attending his yaks and won't be available for many days," the captain said. Very convenient, I thought.

"So we are prisoners now?" Pascal yelled, his face red with anger. "Sophi, tell them that we are leaving in the morning and the hell with his council!"

Captain Little made many smooth apologies and even went out and fetched us a cup of sugar from his own private hoard, but Pascal sat on his bed and stared stonily at the wall, refusing to speak or answer any questions. After a while the four men, showing some embarrassment, left.

We quickly made plans. The next day we would hike with our packs as full as possible along the trail and make a cache of our heaviest food. The day after we would get up about 1:00 A.M. and hike rapidly toward the south, leaving a note saying we were fed up with everything and were heading back to Menkung. When we reached the edge of the Irrawaddy where the trail to Menkung entered the mountains, Pascal and Sophi would continue on south to the river to where our food was stashed, and I would continue to make tracks up the trail for about half a mile, to where the trail got rocky. Afterward I would return and cover our tracks from where we left the main trail. We would then continue down the river, eating our heaviest food first. We hoped to reach the Drung valley before our provisions ran out. I was delighted we were finally going to take matters into our own hands.

SIX

A Terrible Shame

IN A FEW hours, Pascal cooled down and began having second thoughts. We should wait four days, he said, and see if the porters actually come through. I didn't believe the stories we were told and felt we should leave now while it was still easy. Pascal insisted we could "escape" any time, and as long as there was a chance of doing things with the blessing of the military and the locals, we had to wait and see.

We argued half the night but finally went to sleep without resolution. I woke up before the sun, angry and frustrated, and after dressing in warm clothes went out into a field and sat on a rock. I thought again about taking my third of the food and leaving the expedition. I told Sophi as much when she came out to wash her hands and face. Awhile later Pascal came out. "Why don't you leave?" he said, taking me completely by surprise. "But only for a few days. Take Sophi with you, if you want, and go up high into the mountains where the yak herds are. I know you are disappointed that we didn't go up there on the way. You can go away for a few days and both of us can think, and when you come back, we can talk again." He reached out and gave me a rough hug, and there were tears in his eyes. I decided then that if we could resolve these problems without losing our friendship, maybe it would be worth it.

PASCAL'S IDEA FOR me to go up into the mountains was the best one he'd had in a long time. I packed my sleeping bag and raincoat in a fanny pack, along with an extra pile pullover, and prepared to leave. Sophi declined my half-hearted invitation to come; she could sense I wanted to go alone. I took only one Power Bar and a pound of potatoes because it was understood we had to conserve all of our extra food for the trip ahead.

The sun came out and shone brightly for the first time in five days. As upset as I was, I still admired the stark beauty of the high valleys and forests. For eight hours straight I walked as fast as I could up the trail, pausing only briefly to take a few pictures with Pascal's Nikon. Deep in the forest I met a man dressed entirely in yak furs collecting mushrooms in a bamboo basket. In another place, just before the trail crossed the Irrawaddy River, I came to a piece of water-worn limestone that looked very much like a human skull. Someone had lugged it up to the edge of the trail and placed many prayer flags on small bamboo poles in a hole in the top.

Farther up, the Irrawaddy split, and I took the smaller fork, which wound higher into the mountains. Steep lime-stone canyons gave way to sparsely wooded U-shaped glac-ier-etched valleys. Here I started encountering yaks and herders. A kindly middle-aged man with a limp greeted me at the trail and invited me into his family's small cabin for butter tea and tsampa. In the smoky interior his much younger wife laboriously poured yak milk back and forth between three cedar barrels. Inside the barrels, butter col-lected on coiled-up strips of bamboo. Over the fire hung a huge iron cauldron of simmering cheese curds and whey, and in one corner of the room the couple's new baby slept, wrapped in coarse yak-hair blankets. The man indicated food that would be dinner later on, and I knew I was welcome to stay and eat with them, but I was also anxious to climb as high as I could before dark, so I moved on.

Climbing higher into the sparsely wooded valleys that were now stained red in the evening sun, I passed many people who were out milking yaks and shearing sheep. Children screamed and giggled as they chased the sheep down and tied up their legs. (They were having great fun, and I was reminded of greased-pig chases at the Idaho fairs.) Then a strong man held the critters still while a woman, always a woman, carefully cut the wool away with a long Tibetan dagger. I paused for a moment to watch one of the shearings and loaned an old lady one of my razor-sharp, homemade, stainless-steel knives. It was much sharper than the dagger she was using, and only reluctantly did she give it back when I decided to continue on.

Everywhere people seemed to be excited and happy. It was the season of plenty, harvest time, when food must be prepared and stored against the long winter months ahead. Half the village stayed up here tending yaks, making butter and cheese, and shearing sheep, while the rest of the people busily harvested the barley in the lower valleys. Soon the snows would come and the yaks would have to be moved down, where they would quickly eat up any barley that remained in the fields.

I left the people and climbed the rest of the way over a low pass that, as I had hoped, dropped me again into the main fork of the Irrawaddy. Here I expected to find many people, and I anticipated a good dinner of tea, tsampa, and yak-cheese balls. To my surprise and great disappointment, there was no sign of anyone for as far as I could see up the valley. There were only a few small, log, summer cabins, obviously deserted, as no smoke came through the roofs.

A beautiful glacier-capped mountain range rose directly in front of me. This was my goal, the arc of ice-capped peaks that spring out of the Nu-Brahmaputra divide, enclosing the headwaters of the Irrawaddy. But without extra food, I knew I would never reach it. I regretted my haste in not eating with the people in the previous valley and obtaining extra food. Not wanting to turn back, I began hiking up the valley, resigning myself to a night without supper.

In the mountains of Tibet everything appears closer and distances seem much less than they actually are. What appeared to be a small hill, maybe an hour's walk across the valley, turned out to be a large mountain, and after three hours I hadn't even reached the middle of the valley. Thunderclouds that had been building in the west all evening finally overtook me, and it began to pour. I stopped at several small deserted log shanties, but the interiors were filthy and there was no wood for a fire. I couldn't bring myself to cut up the frame boards for firewood, knowing the great effort that had been made to build and carry them up here.

I pushed on through the rain, hoping to find something better. There was a brief break in the storm, and for an instant I thought I saw smoke rising from the roof of a small shanty high up on the opposite side of the valley. After crossing the river on a rickety log bridge, I found a badly eroded livestock trail paved in soggy yak manure that led me to the little building. Several yaks huddled against the walls of the building for shelter against the storm, and yes, there definitely was a thin waft of smoke coming from the roof. Oh, a warm, dry place to spend the night! I called out a greeting in Chinese. A young man cracked open the door and stepped out into the rain. He blinked sleepily several times, then his mouth dropped open. His eyes bugged out and he retreated back into the house and started to shut the door.

"No, no," I pleaded, then realized that, dressed from head to toe in rain gear, with my fluorescent blue balaclava narrowed so there was just a small slit for my eyes, I must have appeared quite the specter indeed. I threw back the hood of my Gore-Tex parka and popped off the hat, at the same time speaking reassuringly to the man in Chinese. He didn't appear to understand, and for the next few minutes stood inside the door staring fearfully at me. Two young children and an old lady also came to the door and regarded me with fear and suspicion. I was hungry and cold, and totally at a loss about what to say or do, and apparently they were also, so we just continued to stare. Finally I pointed to my mouth and chewed, indicating that I was hungry, and reluctantly they let me into the house. Half the floor of the little shanty was covered with rough planks and the other half was dirt. A small silver butter lamp flickering on the red clay hearth was the only ornament in the house. When my eyes adjusted, I counted eleven people. Most had already bedded down in their furs and yak-wool blankets for the night, but now they were waking one another up. A man who seemed to be much older than the one who had let me in roused himself from the floor and then became extremely angry when he realized I was there. He chided the younger man while glaring suspiciously at me out of the corner of his eye. Finally everyone settled down and someone poured me a wooden bowl of butter tea, while someone else brought tsampa and two small barley balls filled with cheese and fried mush-rooms. I ate hungrily, thanking them in Chinese, although none of them seemed to understand. My wet clothes steamed in the heat of the fire, and I was grateful to have shelter. Everyone watched me intently, but no one smiled.

When I had finished eating, the older brother made a large ball of tsampa and gave it to me. He then indicated through gestures that I was to get my things. Puzzled, I put on my fanny pack and followed the younger brother to the door, sure he was taking me to another nearby house to spend the night. To my great surprise and shock he simply said, *"Yamu, yamu"* ("Good-bye") and quickly retreated back into the house, closing the door behind him. I was left standing alone in the pouring rain. Later, when I told Pascal of this incident, he too was greatly shocked, and we agreed that I must have appeared extremely frightening to the people for them to turn me out into such a storm.

The rain was freezing now, and I needed shelter for the night. The only trees up this high were stunted cedars, which alone offered almost no protection against the rain and wind. I hiked a mile or so away from the house but encountered no more buildings, so I decided to build a shel-ter out of cedar trees using my bush knife. I cut trees and limbs and built a small lean-to, then collected handfuls of needles and grass from the base of each of the smaller trees within the vicinity. Shielding this bedding material under my raincoat, I packed it back to my shelter to use as insu-lation beneath me. Finally, I laid my raincoat over this and crawled into my sleeping bag. Outside the storm raged on, but I was almost warm and only a little uncomfortable.

Two stray dogs, of which there are many in Tibet, came down the trail and discovered me. For half an hour they circled around my camp, barking and growling. I had Mace, but if they came that close, I also had my ice ax ready—I was tired and in no mood for harassment. Fortunately for them, they never even came into good rock-flinging range. Finally they left and I slept.

About 4:00 A.M. I was rattled awake by a most ungodly screech. I clung to the shaft of my ice ax, wondering what creature from hell had been sent to torment me this time. Turning on my headlamp, I peered cautiously out into the rain. Only a few yards away, a large gray-and-white yak with one horn turned up and the other turned down stared blindly into the beam. It suddenly let out another unearthly bellow, then sprinted off into the night with an agility and grace I would not have expected.

IN THE MORNING I awoke to find that it was still raining and my down sleeping bag was wet in spite of the shelter. Unless I could dry it somehow, it would be next to useless the following night. I continued to head upstream, eating the ball of tsampa a bite at a time as I went. Rounding a bend, I came upon a village even larger than Ridong. I was on the opposite side of the river, so I crossed a small cantilever bridge to reach it. Several yak hides hanging by wires from the pole railings were agitating in the turbulent water, in some stage of a tanning process, I guessed. Approaching the village, I was, as always, assaulted by several dogs. One particularly ornery mutt came right for me, so I gave him a mouthful of Mace. Several villagers watched from the windows of a house, apparently fascinated by this magic. To them it must have appeared that I had pointed my finger at the dog and sent it into convulsions.

A boy, perhaps fifteen, with a kindly face came out and drove the remaining dogs off with rocks. He immediately invited me into the house. When I indicated that I was hungry, he set a large kettle of rice on the cast-iron cooking stand, then blew the glowing embers of the fire into flames. In the corner the boy's father lay wrapped in coarse yak-wool blankets. At first I thought he was sick, but when I examined him, I found he was injured instead. He had a large bruise and festering wounds over badly broken ribs. I could feel the bones grind when I palpated the area. He was in terrific pain, and I broke our no-medicine rule and gave him a full dose of prescription codeine. I also cleaned the wounds and put antibiotic ointment on them. He seemed grateful, especially half an hour later, when the painkiller took effect.

Many villagers arrived, and they too were curious but kind. By now I had become accustomed to this. They shyly went through my belongings, oohing and aahing and showing one another the strange implements. I resolved that if I ever returned to Tibet, I would bring a whole roll of Velcro.

The boy cooked a huge pot of rice. I thought it must be for everyone, but it turned out that all of it was for me. He melted a pound of fresh butter in it and served me a huge bowlful. I ate until I was stuffed; then he put the rest into one of my plastic bags and handed it to me, also filling my butter can. I left more medicine for the father and gave money to the boy, who walked me back out to the edge of the village. The same ill-tempered dog came running around the corner barking, but as soon as he saw me, he stopped dead in his tracks. The boy watched in wonder as I pointed my finger at the dog and he took off whimpering, tail between his legs.

At the edge of the river I shook the boy's hand warmly and continued on. A 21,000-foot peak, nameless on the maps, loomed directly ahead. My goal was not to climb it, but to reach the beautiful hanging glaciers a third of the way up the lower slopes. I started hiking. For several hours I paced myself, climbing slowly but steadily in the thin air. Suddenly a man dressed in sheepskins and rough wool emerged from the woods below. He screamed and gesticulated, indicating that I was to come down. I didn't know what he wanted, but I'd had about enough of other people telling me what to do the last few weeks, so I turned around and kept going. Shrieking in fury he came after me, shaking his fists and continuing to gesture for me to descend. Here began a strange kind of chase in slow motion. We were about 15,000 feet above sea level, and neither of us could go more than five or ten steps without panting wildly. He followed me for several hundred feet, neither gaining nor falling behind, but finally gave up near the snow line and went down. During this episode it had begun to snow heavily. Cold in spite of my exertion, I decided to give up the glaciers and head back. I traversed half a mile around the base of the mountain before descending, lest I risked encountering the angry Tibetan again.

A long time later I reached a large deserted valley. I hiked through it, then found an enticing camping spot with a pile of wood left by previous travelers. I had plenty of time, so I built a weatherproof shelter from spruce limbs hung on a pole frame set up against a large tree. It took several hours to get the soaked wood hot enough to burn by itself. I cut spruce branches and dried them over the fire, then cut the smaller boughs off and spread them out inside the shelter several inches deep to form a thermal barrier between me and the damp ground. I dried my clothes, boots, and finally my sleeping bag, which, through much care and effort, I managed not to burn. While I worked, I boiled tiny potatoes, five at a time, in my steel cup. When everything was done, I ate the potatoes with large chunks of yak butter, and even without salt it was a delicious meal. I heated up some of the rice the boy had given me and ate that too.

I was full, everything was dry, and I sleepily crawled into the fluffy, warm down sleeping bag. As if a final reward for all this work, the clouds cleared away for several hours and the full moon rose high into the cold, black sky. Tomorrow I would go back to Ridong. I felt a sinking feeling as I contemplated again being under the thumb of Pascal and the military. Somehow I had been happier during these few days alone than on the whole rest of the trip with Sophi and Pascal. I pushed these thoughts out of my mind and snuggled deeper into my bag. It was the first of October. The stars were greatly dimmed by the brightness of the moon, but still I could discern familiar constellations in the crystal-clear sky. They were the same stars I could see in Idaho, and their familiarity suddenly made me feel that the world was actually a very tiny place, that I was not so far from home.

PASCAL MET ME near the village the next day and we had a good talk, although we didn't resolve our differences. On our way back, we were invited by a Tibetan family for tea and tsampa. When we finally arrived at the military base, I ran up and gave Sophi a hug, surprised at how much I'd missed her. I broke out a pound or two of cheese that the villagers had given me. We salted it and began eating. Although it was a lot of cheese, between the three of us we finished it in minutes. We were so hungry for high-calorie foods like cheese and butter!

After dinner I walked outside and just happened to glance through an open door near the captain's quarters. Inside a young soldier sat pedaling frantically on what looked to be a stationary bike. A second soldier was tapping rapidly on a small metal key. Upon seeing me, they stopped suddenly, and one of them jumped up to shut the door.

"Pascal, Sophi, they have a pedal generator and a radio!" I said, bursting into the room. Sophi's face dropped, but Pascal didn't show any sign of surprise. He'd known all along.

WE LEARNED ON October 3 that we weren't going to the Drung valley. The two captains and a man we had not seen before informed us that higher authorities had been summoned from the north to decide what to do with us. The man said we were in a closed military area without proper authorization and that, in his mind, it was amazing we had made it here in the first place. He went on to say that it was his duty to search us and confiscate our film. Pascal acted shocked and outraged at this news, which greatly embarrassed the military officials. We got around the search by sheepishly pulling out several canisters of film and handing them over. These were decoy rolls, of course, and when the men left we carefully hid the rest of our rolls, some in the flour and rice, others outside. We were not sure when the authorities from the north would arrive, but we found out they were supposed to have been there that day. The military captains had been stalling us for the eight days it took a messenger to get to Chyu and back with them.

Pascal still adamantly believed he could use his grand-father story to convince the arriving officials to allow us to continue to the lower Irrawaddy. I was less than optimistic, but if anyone could do it, Pascal could.

We were still having to cook two extra meals ourselves each day, which cut into our precious rations. Sophi over-heard a conference between the two captains in which they were seriously discussing how they were going to ration the food so they wouldn't run out again before the next ship-ment. Later that evening Captain Little grabbed an AK-47 and sprinted out of the complex. I was curious, so when he returned, I asked Sophi to ask him for me what he was after. He replied that since Dr. Liu's service time was up and he was leaving, he had agreed to allow his dog to be shot for meat. However, the animal, seeming to sense that his number was up, had become extremely evasive the last sev-eral days. He told me this with the same big smile that was perpetually glued to his mug, and I started laughing. When both of them stared at me in surprise, I stopped. "Wade," Sophi explained, "that was not a joke."

The police arrived the next morning. Sophi saw them first and ran in to tell us. "Shit, shit," Pascal swore. I went out to see the two men, who were wearing green uniforms with GONG'AN (Police) written on a patch on their right shoulders. They both had small carbines slung across their backs and a special insignia on their uniforms that read, in English, BORDER DUTY.

After they rested in the captain's quarters and had lunch, we were called in for a "discussion." Pascal had sensed this was coming and had conveniently disappeared. Later he told me, "They make me wait for ten days! The least I can do is make them wait a few hours!"

Sophi and I went to the interrogation without him. The two policemen, who were Tibetans, were polite but went right to the point. "You three are in a closed military area illegally. We are here to arrest you, transport you by horse to Chyu, the main city of this county, and from there you will be processed and deported to Sichuan Province in China."

When Pascal finally arrived, he still tried with much energy to talk the policemen into giving us authorization to travel down the Irrawaddy River. Captain Little suddenly piped up and said, "But of course, in Chyu you will be able to get proper authorization to return and then I will provide porters and an armed escort." He smiled his oily grin. This was the last straw for Pascal. He exploded and told Captain Little what he thought of him, through Sophi, in front of the two policemen and others in the room. "Why," he screamed, "have we continually been lied to? Why, when we first arrived, were we told we would get porters in two days—then three—then four? Why then, after that, did you tell us the officials were coming to bring us authorization and porters?" (The captain had said as much the night before.) Pascal continued his barrage, railing on at the man, and by now I knew him well enough to understand that he really was angry, that this was not an act. The captain took the verbal abuse without the least show of concern, carefully answering each of Pascal's questions, giving long, feathery explanations. He talked as if indulging a petulant child. There was absolutely no logic to what he said, but phrases like "Of course, acting with your safety and convenience in mind, we have taken the liberty to . . ." were repeated so many times Sophi got tired of translating them and started saying "Just more bullshit" after each sentence. Pascal had been beaten at his own game.

When the tedious interview finally ended, the two policemen followed us back to our room. They sat on Sophi's bed and stalled for a while before we made them come right out and tell us they wanted to search our things. Furious, Pascal stomped out of the room, which greatly embarrassed the men. Then they systematically, though not thoroughly, began going through our packs. This was fine, since there was nothing in them we wanted to hide. Then the younger of the two started pawing his way down into a twenty-pound sack of potatoes, in the bottom of which Pascal had hidden forty rolls of exposed film. My camera bag was sitting beside me, so I suddenly knocked it off the bed, let out a yell, and caught it before it hit the floor. The policeman paused, looked up, dropped a handful of potatoes back into the sack, and ambled over to see what was so important about the bag. I opened it up to let him see the camera, and he seemed to understand. Fortunately, he never got around to digging in the potatoes again.

WE WERE DOWN to the wire now. There were only two choices: go back to Chyu or try to escape and continue the expedition. If we went back, the expedition was over. Even in the highly unlikely event that they would give us authorization and porters, there would not be enough time to return to Ridong, travel to the lower Irrawaddy, take our pictures, and get out before the first snows of winter closed the passes. But if we escaped and were caught, Pascal told us, we would be in a lot of trouble. He said we would almost certainly be kicked out of China and perhaps never allowed to return. This probably wasn't true, but it was enough to frighten Sophi, as China was her life and career. I was surprised and skeptical, since Pascal was usually the last to take the Chinese authorities seriously.

As the evening wore on, his mood deteriorated and he became sarcastic about every suggestion and angry at the least provocation. He sat stonily on his bed, his back against the crumbly clay wall, staring off into space, the wheels of his mind turning as he tried vainly to resolve the situation. There was no third choice, though; we either left or we didn't. I suspected that defying the authorities through escape was not what he was worried about. He was afraid of the wilderness. So badly had he wanted porters that he'd allowed the captain to string him along for nine days with empty promises and lies. That wouldn't happen to someone like Pascal without a pretty good reason. I realized that throughout this expedition, as well as during our previous trip together, this basic difference in our strategies had repeatedly manifested itself. Regardless of his claims to the contrary, Pascal needed to know that the road ahead was safe and that someone would guide him through. I, on the other hand, couldn't wait for the chance to tear off alone into uncharted territory.

In order to get my cooperation, Pascal had promised earlier that if it came down to escaping, I would have the final say on our route to the Drung valley. However, he vetoed my first plan, which was to leave the main trail and cross into the mountains in the west, eventually following the west fork of the Irrawaddy. I believed that if we went this way, there was little chance they could catch us, as we would leave no footprints in the deep forest duff and there would be no way to predict which direction we had gone in. He insisted we had to follow the main trail downstream.

We had just started packing when a soldier came and announced we were to have dinner with the village chief, the military captain, the two police officers, and some others. We had to keep up a good front so they wouldn't suspect we weren't going to cooperate—at least *I* hoped we weren't.

At dinner Captain Little became pretty well soused and went off on long, sentimental orations about his philosophy of life and how it related to our stay here in Ridong and on and on, with Sophi dutifully translating each line as "More bullshit." He had each of us offer a toast, but when it was Pascal's turn, he refused. He was still seething about the whole situation. For the rest of the evening, there was a sort of power struggle between the two men. The captain was determined that Pascal would toast him before the evening was over, while Pascal adamantly refused.

Also present at the dinner were Ridong's two doctors: Dr. Liu, who had just finished his one year of service and was planning to leave with the police and us the next morning, and Dr. Yu, who had just arrived a few weeks before to take his place. Dr. Liu was twenty-nine, my age, and seemed like a decent man. In a moment of drink-inspired honesty he raised his glass and announced that he was so sorry for what was happening to us and regretted that we had come to Ridong in the first place. It was the only time in nine days I could remember when someone had spoken candidly about our situation.

Pascal finally rose to leave. Captain Little jumped up and blocked his way, holding out a mug of jiu. His face flushed from the alcohol, a grin plastered across it, he again implored Pascal to toast him. I thought Pascal was going to do something violent, but instead, reaching deep within, he managed a tight little smile, said a few words that Sophi translated, then offered the mug back to the captain and stalked out of the room.

When we returned to our room, we quickly finished packing. We were going to try to escape. It was late, but we needed to prepare more food. We had already cooked a chicken and it was soaking in brine. Sophi and I boiled a pot of potatoes. She had bought a side of bacon, which was much too heavy to carry, so we cut it into thin strips and fried it down. Pascal was in an even more wretched mood by now, so after he got his things together, he crawled off to bed, screaming at us twice because we kept him awake with our cooking.

WE AROSE AT 1:30 A.M. and lit one candle to pack by. Sophi and I had gotten less than two hours of sleep. Pascal's disposition hadn't improved, and he snapped furiously at Sophi when she asked him to be more quiet. After that he stuffed a few things around, making more noise, and dropped his flashlight, which bounced loudly on the floor. It was a wonder the whole camp didn't wake up.

After eating breakfast, we blew out the candle and quietly slipped into the night. Sophi left a note near the door saying we were "fed up and going back to Menkung, where the authorities were at least honest." Pascal mumbled that leaving the note was a stupid idea.

It was a beautiful, clear night with an almost-full moon. Pascal led us through the fields up to the first village. Instead of sneaking around, we went directly through the village. Pascal had found the dogs were actually more ferocious when we tried avoiding them by going around. We were hardly bothered at all, although we kept our Mace canisters ready just in case. After two and a half hours and three villages, we arrived at the confluence of the small river that we'd followed out of the mountains ten days before.

I wrapped my boots in heavy cloth and, while Sophi and Pascal waited, went back and erased with a pine limb all our tracks crossing the tiny bridge. I then took off the cloth and made several hundred yards of tracks along the main trail to Menkung. The thick, claylike mud would hold the tracks for several days, even in the constant rain. When I reached a rocky area where no tracks would be left, I retreated, walking backward and occasionally taking an extra step so there appeared to be three sets of tracks. Our boots all had waffle soles, which were unlike any Tibetan shoes, so I hoped this ruse, along with the note, would throw off pursuers for a while.

From here I wanted to cross the mountains to the west toward the other fork of the Irrawaddy, but Pascal still wouldn't agree to this. Our only chance of escaping by the main trail we were on was if no one followed us or if we made extremely good time.

I rewrapped my boots and went back to join Sophi and Pascal. Following a good trail down the river, we passed quietly through a camp of sleeping Tibetans. Fortunately, they didn't have dogs. I carefully erased our tracks for the first few hundred yards, then gave up the effort as being too time-consuming. After we crossed the bridge, I began to feel better. It seemed as though the noose that had been tightening around our necks had suddenly loosened, and I felt free. Pascal and Sophi, however, had a tough time of it, as they hadn't done any significant hiking for ten days. I had gotten out four of the days and had even been up to 15,000 feet, so I felt fit. We were still around 12,000 feet, and each of us had a lot of extra weight, with the twelve days' worth of food we were carrying. Sophi had to stop often to catch her breath, and twice she fell badly. Even so, she didn't complain.

After a short distance, the trail became narrow, and Pascal suggested it was so dangerous that we should stay there and wait for morning. There was a full moon and I thought what he said was ridiculous, so I pushed on, and reluctantly he followed. At 7:30 A.M. Pascal insisted he and Sophi couldn't hike any further. I was sure we had a six-hour head start and I wanted to go at least three or four more hours, but Pascal whispered that Sophi was beat and he didn't want to push her too hard. I wasn't sure that this wasn't just another of Pascal's excuses, but we left the trail and followed a small stream up into the woods. In a se-cluded, flat spot protected from the rain by a giant spruce tree, we set up camp. We were much too close to the trail, and I begged Pascal to go on, but again I could not change his mind. I felt my resentment of Pascal growing. It built in my chest until I wanted to scream, to hit something. I felt like scooping up my pack and taking off alone. But Pascal had power over me. He knew it and I knew it, and it gave him final say in everything.

Once more I went back to cover our tracks in hopes of misleading any searchers. At a very early age, my father had taught me how to read tracks and animal signs—a skill essential to hunting in the mountains. His quiet words of explanation and instruction filtered into my mind as the trail ahead told its story of the past few days. Yesterday two men had passed this way, traveling downstream together, one of them leading a heavily laden pack animal. Later that evening a large buck deer had followed the same direction, pausing briefly to feed on the delicate foliage in several places. From the depth and spacing of the tracks, he appeared to be favoring his left hind leg. When I reached the spot where we had left the main trail, I paused again briefly and examined the telltale smudges in the mud where I had smoothed out our tracks, then worked methodically to obliterate even these minor signs of our passing before returning to our camp. I felt good about my work. I just hoped there weren't any skilled trackers among the Tibetans around here.

SOPHI AND PASCAL slept most of the day, and I should have slept too, but I was uneasy about where we were. We had planned to hole up somewhere for three days, until the military gave up looking for us, then continue downriver, but not here. I urged Pascal to let us move on and find a more secluded spot, but he proposed a compromise. We could make a sort of mud trap for footprints by smoothing out a section of the trail. If no one crossed it that day, or if they did and the tracks indicated that they had returned, we would head out again early the next morning. Reluctantly I went up the trail and made the mud trap.

It was a great feeling to finally be out from under the thumb of the military. I just hoped we could stay free! Because I couldn't sleep, I inventoried our food. We had six days' worth of freeze-dried dinners, thirty-six Power Bars, ten pounds of powdered milk, around three and a half pounds of yak butter, six pounds of buckwheat noodles, seven pounds of rice, six packs of instant ramen noodles, about a pound of dried yak meat, five very small potatoes, a pound of tsampa, and nine pounds of canned meat. Since entering Tibet, I had seldom had a full stomach. The constant exertion, coupled with the high altitude, meant that I was burning a tremendous number of calories. In addition, the uncertainty of finding food necessitated some rationing. Pascal controlled our rations with an iron fist, and I usually didn't know when we were finally going to eat, or how much we would get. As a result, I was hungry all the time and found a large part of my thinking devoted to food.

The forest was beautiful. We had pitched our tent on a carpet of undergrowth so lush and soft we didn't need to blow up the air mattresses. Later in the evening, Sophi and I sat together under the giant spruce tree and softly sang Pink Floyd songs. Pascal went by himself down to the stream to write in his journal.

"What do you think is going on with him?" I asked Sophi after a while.

"I'm not sure," she answered, then added thoughtfully, "You know, it's almost like he wanted to get caught this morning. He really made a lot of noise; I was furious! And then the fire when we got here."

When I had returned from covering the signs of our passing, I had found Pascal had started a big, smoky fire. He had been almost contemptuous of me when I had insisted on putting it out after breakfast.

"You know, Wade," Sophi said after a while, "we are probably not going to make it to the Drung people." After traveling over a hundred miles across one of the most topographically rugged regions of South Tibet, we were only twenty miles from where we could expect to find them. We were so close, and the statement should have sounded crazy, but I knew she was right. Somehow I could feel that Pascal was simply never going to let us get there. If I wanted to see the Drung valley, I would have to go by myself. Anyway, we were free now and that night, at least, we would sleep in the forest.

The sun shone steadily. The forest had become strangely quiet. There were only soft little birdcalls. I picked up the pot in which Sophi had made noodles and got up lazily. Suddenly a single rifle shot exploded, and a bullet whizzed through the branches over my head. I wheeled around swearing as Sophi sprang to her feet. Three more quick shots rang out and a man dressed in camouflage rose from the bushes on the side of the canyon above. He leveled his AK-47, and a burst of rifle fire ripped through the trees above, showering us with wood chips and pine boughs. "Get down, Sophi!" I screamed, grabbing her arm. We both dove onto the ground behind the trunk of the huge spruce we were camped under. Then I heard the shrill voice of Captain Little.

"He's telling us to get up," Sophi translated.

"The hell with that," I exclaimed, crouching even closer to the tree. I heard something behind me and turned to see Pascal slowly walking up the bank, hands held high above his head. I could also see six men to our right with guns trained on him and us. Sophi yelled up to Captain Little that we were getting up, to please not shoot us. He advanced down the hill, rifle held at ready, eyes blazing with fury. Behind him the hill came alive as scores of Tibetan woodsmen, along with a few soldiers, rose from hiding places in the foliage. It reminded me of a movie where the director has been filming a quiet, intimate scene with two characters in a secluded and private place, then suddenly the camera zooms back to reveal a large studio audience.

Captain Little paused to snap a new thirty-round clip into his rifle. "What a shame." Sophi translated his words. "What a terrible shame! We treated you as friends, but you are not our friends. You are bad people and deserve to have something very bad happen to you."

SEVEN

The Price of the Butter

THERE WERE TEN or twelve soldiers and villagers gathered around us in a semicircle, guns pointed at our chests. More and more people began to materialize out of the foliage. Some were villagers from Ridong, others were woodsmen—Tibetans who make a living by cutting firewood and hunting rare predators for pelts. These men all carried large, silver-handled daggers in their belts and large bush knives on their backs. The two policemen were also there. One of them gave a pair of handcuffs to a young Tibetan villager, who dutifully handcuffed Pascal to me. He was apparently unfamiliar with the device and squeezed the cuff so tightly I thought my wrist bones would break. Again the captain's voice rang out. "You deserve to have something very bad happen to you. Sophi," he commanded, "come here." She obeyed and walked stiffly out of the semicircle, leaving Pascal and me alone. The captain yelled another command and each of the men threw a shell into the chamber of his rifle. Most of the men had already chambered a shell, and so ejected an unfired round out onto the ground. At the next command, they dropped a small lever down on the right side of their rifles, making them fully automatic. Earlier in the week I had gotten to examine one of the guns, and so I knew what was going on.

"Pascal, does this look like a firing squad to you?" I whispered.

"Shut up!" he hissed back. "Don't move. Don't speak to me. I don't think they would shoot us on purpose. They are just trying to scare us!" They were succeeding. The rifles were set at a one-kilogram (2.2-pound) trigger pull, one of the soldiers had informed me proudly in a conversation a few days before. I realized that if one of the men sneezed, we could get cut in half.

The captain yelled out several more commands or threats to us; I wasn't sure which, because Sophi was gone. Then, to my horror, he marched cockily behind the row of men, did a precision about-face, and fired his rifle into the air. Both of the Tibetans in the lineup and one of the soldiers visibly flinched, and we were lucky not to be shot by accident.

"This guy is crazy!" I whispered to Pascal. "He is out of control!"

"He's an asshole!" was the reply.

I'm not sure what would have happened next, but suddenly the older of the two Tibetan policemen took charge of the situation, boldly stepping between us and the guns, and began checking us for weapons. Next they roughly searched our packs, carelessly dumping the contents onto the ground. Pascal's camera bag was flung open, and all the equipment roughly shaken out in a pile.

Sophi came back—they had taken her to collect our tent—and the captain took advantage of her presence to berate us more.

"You came here to find trouble. Now you have it! You think you can do as you please here, but here I am in authority, and you will find that everyone obeys me!"

By this time my hand had turned dark blue, as had Pascal's; mine was numb. Through Sophi, I asked if the policeman would loosen the handcuffs, and he agreed to take them off, but they were squeezed so tightly that at first the teeth would not disengage with the key. He finally had to squeeze the cuffs even tighter to get them to release. The blood rushed back into my fingers with an excruciating sensation.

We were told to repack our things for the hike back to Ridong. For the first time since they had arrived, I began to recognize individual soldiers and villagers as the people I had come to know in the previous days. Dr. Liu stood near me holding a submachine gun. He had been the only one of the men carrying guns to disobey the order to point them at us. I saw tears in his eyes. On my other side was a young boy of about fifteen whose family had invited me over for dinner four times in the last two weeks. Now he refused to look at me. One of the woodsmen hoisted Sophi's pack onto his shoulders, oblivious to the straps; Pascal and I were both required to carry ours. We climbed up the hill and followed game paths back down toward the main trail on the river. Carefully hidden beside the path were small burlap sacks tied shut with leather thongs, which the Tibetans retrieved as we hiked along. Inside each were tsampa, butter, cheese, and small sticks of pitch wood for starting fires. Each of the villagers and woodsmen had one of these, which they had stashed before the final sneak into our camp. They had been prepared to hike for days.

I was afraid they would find and confiscate my film, which I'd hidden in my sleeping bag, so after a couple of hours, I threw my pack down and pretended something was poking my back. I did this several times, punching the backpack and pretending to get angrier and angrier. Finally I ripped out my sleeping bag, opened it, and dropped a lot of things on the ground, including my film, behind my pack. I used the sleeping bag to pad the imaginary pointed spot from the inside, picked up the film and the backpack in the same motion, and later, when I was a little ahead of the group, zipped the rolls into my raincoat pocket.

It was a grueling hike back, but we munched Power Bars and pushed on. As we walked, more Tibetans came down out of the canyons and trees, each with a large bush knife and a small sack of provisions. As we neared the army camp in Ridong, I began to take frequent breaks to use the bathroom. When they asked what my problem was, I had Sophi tell them I was getting diarrhea again.

When we reached the fork of the Irrawaddy, even more Tibetans came out of the trees. There were well over a hundred in all and I realized that we hadn't stood a chance of getting away. Back at the military camp, a big bonfire burning brightly in the flooded basketball court cast eerie shadows over the faces of thirty or so more Tibetans and the few soldiers who gathered around it. I quickly dropped my pack and bolted for the field where the toilet was located. No one paid any attention or followed. I buried the film under a heavy rock and returned. The young Tibetan soldier who was also the cook was busy preparing noodle soup in six large cauldrons balanced between burning logs. Apparently the villagers had brought them in for the occasion. Soldiers quickly carried our packs into the room we had occupied for nine days. It was nearly 1:00 A.M., just twenty-two and a half hours since we had left.

I went back outside to warm by the fire and forty pairs of unfriendly eyes watched me approach. Someone brought a bench and someone else set a cup of steaming tea beside me, but that was all. No one spoke or smiled as I sipped a little of the butter tea. Yes, we had broken the law. Yes, we had been caught. I shouldn't have been angry. But I was— so angry I couldn't hold it in. Suddenly I rose and kicked the bench as hard as I could, sending it into the fire. The cup of tea also flew into the flames with a loud hiss. Several men started toward me, but I turned on them with my fists and they backed off. Someone screamed for Sophi, and she came running. As I stared into the stonelike faces of the villagers and woodsmen, many of whom had been our friends only a day before, fury rose up in me again and I kicked the fire, spilling two of the cauldrons of noodle soup. Sophi came and asked calmly, "Wade, what is going on?"

"He almost killed us!" I screamed. "That little son of a bitch shot at us when he knew we had no guns!" Sophi translated this to several soldiers standing nearby as I hauled off and kicked another bench, feeling the wood splinter under my boot. Pascal arrived and tried to calm me down. Although I was angry at him too, I felt some control return, but it still infuriated me to see all the expressionless Tibetans staring at us.

It was Pascal who broke the spell. He opened a carton of cigarettes and solemnly began passing them around the circle of men. In a moment I grabbed several packs and did the same. Eyes that had been narrowed in distrust opened wide in surprise, and some of the kindness returned to the faces of the men, including the village chief.

Captain Little came out of one of the rooms and entered his own quarters. Like a predator I watched him from across the exercise yard as he took off his shoulder holster and hung it on the wall. A little later he came out, locked the door, and walked toward the fire. To me it appeared he was strutting, and cold fury overtook me again. I moved backward to a position that kept me hidden behind a large Tibetan woodsman. When the captain stepped around the man into the firelight, a big, oily smile plastered on his face, I stiff-armed him in the chest so hard his head snapped forward and he stumbled back out of the circle, almost falling in the mud. With a look of confusion and surprise, he reached for his pistol. "You don't have it, do you?" I screamed in English, bearing down on him. He back-pedaled but was off balance, and I had the jump on him. I took two quick steps and launched a kick to his groin, but strong hands caught me by the shoulders, and I missed by inches. I wheeled around and found myself face-to-face with Captain Big. Swearing in rage I fought to tear loose, but his eyes pierced through my anger as he said in broken English, "Please, we are very sorry. Stop please." His hands were like vises, and I couldn't shake him loose. Two soldiers grabbed Captain Little and quickly marched him into his room. As I struggled to rip free and go after him, Pascal showed up, grabbed me, and dragged me into our room. He barred the door and pleaded with me to stay inside and sleep the night.

Food was brought to us, a lot of food. The military also fed the fifty Tibetans who spent the rest of the night around the bonfire. Outside I heard men talking and even a little laughter. Then someone started playing a slow Tibetan song on a Chinese fiddle, and a little later someone else joined in with a harmonica. Soon after that I slept. I dreamed again of shooting the huge buck with my father, and of the shadowy, ravenlike bird slowly descending toward me as I galloped a frenzied pony across the Tibetan plateau.

THE NEXT MORNING we were brought breakfast. Outside, the bonfire still roared and the young cook dutifully fed the thirty Tibetans milling around. I wondered if the military would be reimbursed for these lost rations, knowing as I did how little food they had available. Captain Big showed up to discuss my violent outburst. He said that there had been a terrible misunderstanding, that Captain Little had not fired at us but had only shot three times in the air to signal the other men to come. This again infuriated me, and I raged at him. I'm not sure how much Sophi translated, but the captain gave us a cup of sugar he said Captain Little had sent, then left.

Before lunch, when I saw Captain Little himself come out of his room and head for the latrine field, I grabbed Pascal's walking stick and set out on a collision course. Pretending not to see me, he quickly turned around and went back into his room. Quite a few soldiers and Tibetans witnessed this incident. Humiliating him felt good. Later I would not be so proud of myself.

Arrangements were made with two packers for nine horses to carry us and our things north to the nearest road. There was no more discussion of our escape, and Pascal and I retrieved our film from hiding places outside.

In late afternoon Captain Little himself came to our room, quickly deposited an armload of canned beef on the table as a gift, said repeatedly that he was sorry, then hurriedly left before I could attack him. Still later a soldier came and pleaded with Sophi to talk to the captain so she could then talk to me and make peace between us before we left. We consented, and she went off. Captain Little began by explaining to Sophi how he had been under enormous pressure to find us, and that if he hadn't, it might well have cost him his military career. One of the policemen had heard us leave and a little later had gotten up to check on us. Within a few hours they had organized and started their search, rousing villagers along the way. My false footprints and Sophi's note had worked at first, and they had gone past the bridge, following the trail all the way to the pass. Finding no more footprints and certain that we had not been able to go that far uphill at such an altitude with our heavy packs, they had swept down through the mountains, back toward the Irrawaddy River. Eventually some of the woodsmen had discovered our camp and brought the others there. The soft birdcalls I had heard had been the whistling of Tibetans communicating to each other as they sneaked up on us.

The captain told Sophi to tell me he was terribly sorry for shooting at us, but he was presently under a great deal of stress here in Ridong. He was only twenty-five—just a few months out of the officer-training academy—and this was his first assigned post. Our arrival in Ridong had been particularly stressful for him because he hadn't known how to handle us. It was something he had not been taught, and when we took off, it had greatly frightened and upset him.

After Sophi explained this to me, Dr. Liu and Captain Big came in to discuss the situation. They said a lot of things, but what it boiled down to was that most of the villagers and some of the soldiers hadn't agreed with Captain Little's shooting at us. He had lost a lot of respect through the incident and much more yet when I shoved him and then later intimidated him with the stick. They said that when I got to Chyu, what I told about this incident could have a profound effect on his career.

They asked me to consider that maybe what had happened to him was already enough. Later, after much thought, when I had settled down, I decided to go visit with Captain Little personally. As Sophi and I entered his room, his eyes opened wide, but Sophi assured him we had come in peace. I told him I forgave him, but that I was not willing to speak further about the incident. My intention was that he would no longer worry about what I might say in the future.

When Sophi finished translating, the captain suddenly stepped forward and threw his arms around me. A great sob shook his body, and for a few moments he cried freely. When he finally stepped back, real tears stained my green bush jacket. It was only at this time that I was able to let go of my anger and see things through his eyes. I left with a strange mixture of emotions, but mostly I felt remorse and regret that our presence and actions in Tibet had again caused someone difficulty.

WE ATE LIKE kings the last day in Ridong. Both captains brought armloads of canned meat, and for the first time in twelve days the young Tibetan cook brought more food than we could eat. It seemed that the more trouble we caused, the better we were treated.

We left Ridong on the seventh of October. Two packers and nine animals showed up to carry us and our things north up the Irrawaddy. Besides the packers and our group, there were the two policemen and Dr. Liu, eight people in all. I looked around Ridong one final time. The last horse caravan had brought a new toffeelike candy from Chengdu and a sack of gum-rubber inner tubes. All the village men and half the soldiers had meticulously whittled out slingshots and were busy terrorizing the dogs, pigs, and chickens that were permanent residents of the base. Pascal turned to me and said, "It's really like they are children—children with toys." When he said "toys," I knew he meant their guns, not the slingshots. The real children of the village watched their fathers and older brothers with ill-concealed envy.

A large number of people from the village came to see us off. The occasion was the departure of Dr. Liu, who had served double duty as military doctor and physician for the people of Ridong and the surrounding villages. Captain Little again came forward and gave me a big hug in front of the soldiers, but I felt it was for show only, that the sincerity from the night before was gone.

"One minute he wants to kill you, the next minute he wants to kiss you," Pascal commented dryly.

When we had gone two hundred yards from the camp, we paused and the Tibetans called out a farewell to the villagers who had gathered just beyond the camp. The villagers gave an answering call. The packers called out again, and this time we all joined in, and again the villagers answered. The farewell was repeated a third time, and then we continued on.

THAT EVENING I talked to Pascal about his failure to reach the Drung valley. "How do you feel?" I asked him. "Are you greatly disappointed?"

"No," he answered thoughtfully. "Sometimes you need to do what you can. Then you have to be happy with what you have done. We have had a remarkable trip. We entered this closed area of Tibet and have stayed for over a month. We have gone places where no Westerners have gone in nearly a century and have stayed at places where no one else has been."

"Are you going to make another attempt to reach the Drung valley?"

"No. At least not now. Maybe someday when China is more open, I will come back and try again."

That night it was difficult for me to sleep. In Hong Kong we had discussed the trip in great detail and agreed not to stick our necks out with the authorities. When it came down to it, though, Pascal had just kept walking closer and closer to the edge until finally he had fallen over and gotten us caught. What frustrated me most wasn't that we had failed—indeed, we'd had a remarkable trip and had actually made it farther than I had expected. What upset me was that I'd had no part in the decisions that led to the failure or success. Many times we had disagreed about how to proceed. In the end I was always left with the same two choices: do it Pascal's way or leave the expedition—and he knew I was too loyal to leave. We had brought ropes, climbing equipment, and enough dehydrated food to cross the mountains by ourselves safely, independent of the authorities. This had been our original plan, and a good one. I had brought to the expedition a lifetime of mountain-climbing, survival, and back-country skills. I realized, as I lay under the stars that night, that Pascal would never use me, the equipment, or the food. During the entire expedition Pascal had continually given the responsibility for our safe passage to someone else. Now it was my turn to take responsibility for myself. If I ever wanted to see the Drung valley, I'd have to travel alone.

• • •

AS WE CLIMBED toward the headwaters of the Irrawaddy, the day was clear and warm and the scenery increasingly more spectacular. Sophi and I walked together and compared our perceptions of what had happened. She too was angry at Pascal and disgusted with our situation. "He was afraid," she said vehemently. "And his fear made him fail. He doesn't deserve ever to reach the Drung valley!"

"You know, Sophi, I'm going back to try again." I spoke suddenly, telling her of a decision I had made earlier that morning.

"This year? This trip?" she asked in surprise.

"If I can. If there is a chance. If not, I will come back next year. Sophi, I have to try. Then if I fail, I can be at peace. I'm so tired of being completely controlled."

"Do you realize, Wade, that we still have all the food we bought in Yanjing, plus all the dehydrated food we brought along? I think, even had we made it to the Drung valley and then back to China, we never would have eaten that food. Think about this morning."

She was referring to an incident in which she and I had grabbed a Power Bar out of the food pack and Pascal had told us to "Put that back," that we needed to "save that food!"

Many times during our arguments Pascal had used Sophi as a reason for not doing things my way. *We must stay here several days because Sophi needs a rest! We have to have the horses for Sophi. I think Sophi is afraid to go through the mountains.* I felt it was only fair to confront Sophi with this, since we were ripping Pascal so hard, but to my surprise she denied all of it.

"He hid his fear behind me!" she screamed. "Oh, am I going to have a talk with him!"

Pascal, oblivious to our conversation, was in great spirits. He'd cut a deal with the military police to give them a camera in exchange for allowing us to take photographs of our journey out. He bustled around photographing everything, his face beaming with pleasure. His mood had improved dramatically soon after we had been caught by the police. Earlier I would have been puzzled by this, but now I understood: he knew exactly where we were going and we had someone to guide us through.

THE NEXT MORNING I told Pascal, "You know, I'm going back. I hope you understand. It's not that I am disappointed about our trip. It was wonderful. But I had almost no effect on the success or failure. You controlled, decided, and changed everything. I feel I am one of those survival kits you buy at an army surplus store for twelve dollars— you know, the ones that have matches, a knife, fish hooks, and a signal mirror. You put it in your coat pocket, but of course you never expect to use it. You never used me, Pascal. I don't think you ever planned to. You knew if there was an emergency, well, I was there in your pocket, a walking, living, breathing survival kit, and that was what you wanted, not a human being with opinions and desires of his own. I understand that, and I think I understand you and the way you think. You made a good choice. I'm a well-trained and very resourceful survival kit, but you must understand that for me, that is not enough. I have to do more than just sit in your pocket and wait for an emergency, and that is why I have to go back and try it the way we originally planned. I gave up half a year of my life and all the money I had to come on this expedition. I hope you can understand."

At first Pascal was angry. After all, reaching the Drung valley was his dream, not mine. But a little later, he seemed to get over being upset and approached me. "I have a proposition! I will go with you back to the Drung valley, but we will do it your way, all the way. I don't say a word. I promise I will do it. But there is one thing I want. I want to go through Do-Kar-La-Pass so I can photograph Kar-Kar-Po."

I was not prepared for this offer; I thought that Pascal had given up trying to reach the Drung valley. His new plan would mean traveling sixty more miles down the Yunnan/Tibetan highway, where we'd risk getting caught for a couple more days. I asked Sophi what she thought. She replied, "If you go with him again, I think you will fail again. I don't think he trusts you, Wade. Right now he says he will do this and that, but you know when it gets down to crossing the mountains without a trail or going fifteen hours a day, it will be like before when we tried to escape. It just won't happen. We have a saying in France: You can't have the butter and the price of the butter too. He wants to go to the Drung valley, and now that you are going to leave him, he says he is willing to compromise and do some things your way, except that he actually still wants to do everything his way! Maybe inside he knows this, and that is why he wants to go to Kar-Kar-Po, because then when he fails to reach the Drung valley, at least he will have pictures of the pilgrims to sell." She tossed her head in disdain, and her eyes blazed a reflection of the morning sun. She was beautiful. Emotions swept through me and I searched for courage.

"Sophi, what about me?" She knew what I was asking.

The question hung painfully between us. Stopping she looked directly at me, her face softening in compassion.

"You are my friend, Wade, my dear, dear friend." She grabbed my hands, squeezing them as she spoke. A wave of disappointment washed over me, but at the same time there was release.

Later in the afternoon I approached Pascal and asked him, "If I decide to go back by myself, will it ruin our friendship?" "Yes, of course," he replied, and I felt sick to my stomach. But a little later he turned to me, smiled, and clapped his hand on my shoulder. "You can take one of my cameras."

Instantly I felt my own fears return. I remembered the first time two years ago when I saw the cold, blue steel of a gun and a pair of handcuffs in a policeman's belt and I realized *I was being arrested in Communist China*. Nausea had washed over me and my legs had weakened. I had come a long way since then, but I was still afraid. Without Pascal I would have to confront that fear alone. It would be a big part of really finishing this trip.

PART II

The Sun Is Good, the Sun Is God

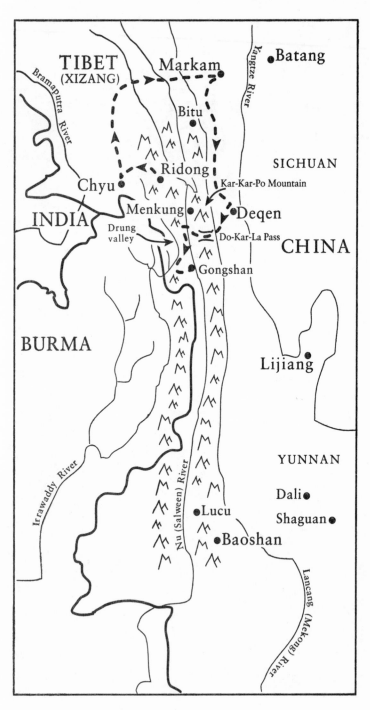

Third (Solo) Journey

EIGHT

Pilgrim's Trail

DOWN, DOWN, DOWN I flew almost at a full run, careening back and forth through the short, steep switchbacks. In the hazy distance the Nu Mountains' snow-dusted passes glimmered portentously in the pale afternoon light. I found myself thinking, This is crazy! It's irresponsible! What are you doing? SHUT UP! Far below I could see four pilgrim women dressed in traditional Tibetan wool and skins and wearing bright blue Chinese hats. They made their way through the high valleys, then disappeared into the trees. Eventually I too reached the forest, and I hiked for several hours along the beautiful trail. At a huge grove of bamboo the path split; the larger fork went south up a canyon while the smaller fork continued downstream. After much deliberation, I took the road less traveled, not because I'd been reading Robert Frost, but because it seemed to be going in the right direction. After a few miles I came to a damp spot and found the footprints of the four women; we were either all on track or wrong together.

Near a stream crossing I stopped for a drink. Here I discovered a skeleton moldering in a bamboo patch. It was dressed in a rotting blue shirt and khaki trousers. A closer examination revealed that it was not a human skeleton but that of a wolf. I found the skull nearby. "Why," I wondered out loud, "would someone dress a wolf carcass in human clothing and leave it for others to find?" Was it part of an obscure Buddhist ritual or only a practical joke? I hurried past.

Just as the day was ending, I found a dry flat spot near the river and quickly set up a shelter with the plastic sheet I had purchased in Chyu (Pascal had taken his tent), then got a hot fire burning. I was carrying four two-pound cans of meat and was anxious to eat these first to be rid of the weight. Two were cans the military had sold us. Afterward, they had come and taken the labels off. Later, the captain had returned all the money. It was mystery mealtime.

One of the cans contained pork and eggs, my favorite Chinese concoction. I also cooked a large pot of rice, enough for three more meals. It was a strange yet tranquil feeling to suddenly be so alone. Although it was still early, the air was freezing cold. I crawled into my sleeping bag and snuggled to get warm. I found myself thinking of Sophi. It had been harder than I thought to say good-bye to her. We had cooked together, eaten together, had been shot at and searched together; we had killed chickens, treated sick villagers, hiked all day in the rain, and sung Pink Floyd songs under our breath by the light of a full moon while attempting to escape the Chinese military, police officers, and a hundred angry Tibetan woodsmen and villagers. After two months of such intensity, you either love your companions or you hate them. Indifference isn't an option.

IT TOOK FOUR days to reach Chyu from Ridong. Chyu wasn't anything like what we had expected, and we started worrying as soon as we saw it. The people of Ridong had described it as a virtual paradise where there was everything a person might want, and for them I guess it might have been, as they had no other city for comparison. But for us, after a month of relative wilderness, the city's huge, forlorn cement installations were less than enticing. It was obvious that Chyu was a military city. We passed lots full of green jeeps and trucks, and at least two-thirds of the people on the streets wore uniforms. The town was divided into two sections. The larger, central part was strictly military, while the periphery was the actual town of Chyu, more a large village than anything else; there were many private houses, a few restaurants, and dozens of little one-room shanty stores. New construction was going on near the police station when we arrived, and we could see pilgrims cooking their meals over log fires within the bare cement walls of the partially completed buildings where they had taken refuge for the night.

We were quickly hustled into the police station by eleven policemen and policewomen. All our possessions were immediately locked in a room, and a large Tibetan man dressed in a suit spoke briefly with the two military border police who had brought us, then dismissed them. When Sophi told the man we were tired and hungry, we were hustled off to a restaurant for dinner. Everyone was extrememly official and efficient, and it scared me.

After dinner they rushed us back to the station for interrogation. The old Tibetan man with his official suit laughed contemptuously when Pascal told his grand-father/explorer story. He was the first person ever to openly disbelieve it, and Pascal was visibly shaken. The man bawled us out through Sophi, and when she tried to explain something, he cut her off and chastened us some more. During this "questioning" I decided I'd better hide my film and told them I urgently neeeded to use the bathroom. Two men took me outside and stood over me with flashlights as I squatted on the ground. It was incredibly humiliating and I seethed with anger. I returned to the interrogation room with the rolls still zipped in the pocket of my raincoat and told Pascal about the incident so he could think of other ways to save our film.

They searched Pascal first but weren't very organized because there were so many people involved. While everyone was oohing and aahing over his inflatable air mattress, he casually picked up his boxes of film and shoved them into his pack. Sophi was next, and she also managed to hide her camera and all her film.

When it was my turn, I hoisted my backpack onto the bench and carefully slid my camera bag, which contained all my unexposed film, under the desk with my foot. They found my journal, though, and some of my maps. Then the official said that they wanted to search our bodies. I was still wearing my raincoat with the film in the pocket, so I quickly took it off and draped it over a chair. Luckily no one checked it.

Suddenly a pencil-thin Chinese man with a constipated look on his face—the only person in the room besides us who didn't seem to be thoroughly enjoying the event— spied Pascal's camera bag. My heart sank as the officers greedily pawed through the assortment of lenses, camera bodies, and flashes. Finally they hauled out his forty rolls of exposed film.

After the search we were taken to a kind of police guest house nearby, but we had to leave our things locked up at the station. Pascal and I managed to carry our camera bags across the courtyard and up to our room; I concealed the small bag under my coat until we were alone. After a few minutes I decided to test our confines and went out to use the bathroom. Sure enough, a policeman waited outside to escort me to and from the squatter, so I decided to wait for a better opportunity to hide my film. The rooms and beds were amazingly clean and comfortable by Chinese standards, and we slept like the dead.

We were questioned individually about our trip the next morning. Since Sophi was the only person who could translate, it was easy to keep the stories straight. Afterward they searched us again, confiscating my journal and the maps they had found the day before. I was distressed and worried about losing my journal, but I managed to steal it back while they were busy checking Sophi. Later I hid it, along with my film, behind the toilet under a large flat rock.

After the first two days the cold-war treatment ended and we were pretty much left alone. We were required to stay in the general vicinity of the police station except at meals, to which we were escorted. I began getting up early to work out before the police or military were out and about. I set aside half an hour each morning to run, do push-ups and chin-ups, and to stretch. My body responded well to the exercise, rest, and good food, and within a week I felt strong and fit. I was in the best aerobic shape I had ever been in and could sprint uphill for hundreds of yards without having to stop and catch my breath. One morning I decided to ignore the rules the police had given us about staying nearby. Before the sun was up I hoisted myself over the fence and went for a long run in the mountains above Chyu. As I dug my feet into the loose shale hillside, my legs pumping like pistons, the exertion burned away the stresses that had been building during the past few days, and my spirits rose with the altitude gain. I jogged for a little over three thousand feet to the base of some massive limestone spires that formed the clustered peak of a mountain near town. Without pausing I began climbing the highest of these. The rock was warm and inviting and my muscles responded as I worked my way to the needle-shaped summit. There, to my astonishment, I found prayer flags rippling in the wind. I marveled at the person who had put them there and wondered if he had brought ladders from below or climbed the rock as I had done. It was a tough climb, but again I couldn't imagine anyone hauling one of those heavy Tibetan notched-log ladders up from the valley below. Either way, I had great admiration for whoever had put the flags there. I took a small pebble from my pocket, placed it beside the flags, and said a prayer to my own god before climbing down.

At the base of the spires a long talus-and-scree slope started that trailed a thousand feet to the trees below. I shot down it in great leaps and bounds, instantly developing reckless speed. Laughing in the cool air, I skidded and skied along a tiny rock avalanche startled up and driven before me. Losing my balance I fell hard once, then scrambled back to my feet just in time to screech to a lurching halt at the bottom of the chute amid massive boulders and stunted cedar trees. Hopping up on a flat boulder I squatted on my haunches and watched the taffy-gold streaks of morning light chase long dark shadows cast by the rising sun emerging from behind the ragged peaks that rose in the west. I felt a vitality I hadn't known for years. I thought of that sunny day in September playing football when I had lost it. But that was ten years ago, and now I was whole and strong, glowing. I knew it then: it was right to go back. This was a journey I needed to finish.

ON SATURDAY THE sixteenth of October, a telegram came through from Lhasa. We were to be released and transported by truck to Sichuan. No fine was to be imposed, and our things were to be returned to us. The military issued permits that allowed us to travel out of the closed area.

The only thing they refused to return was my large Tibetan machete. This was upsetting because I definitely needed one for building shelters and making fires, and it would be hard to replace. I kept insisting that they would have to pay for it, and finally it was returned to me.

We boarded trucks and traveled back to Markam where our journey had started near the border of Sichuan Province. Here Sophi left us and went on alone to Chengdu, then back to France. The soldiers in charge of us simply turned us loose at Markam, and we found that our permits allowed us to travel with impunity through the restricted areas. A few days later Pascal and I reached Do-Kar-La, a sacred pass in the Kar-Kar-Po Mountains nearly a hundred miles south of where we had originally crossed the Nu-Lancang divide. Here Pascal photographed pilgrims who were circling a massive glacier-etched peak in hopes of obtaining a better rebirth in the life to come. It was here, amidst a thousand prayer flags, that I chose to leave Pascal and finish my journey alone.

"You know, Wade," Pascal said, as he put his camera away, "you could always go with me to Vietnam. I am going there as soon as I get back to Hong Kong. I am going to find a beautiful woman and have the *real* vacation."

"I can't Pascal. You know I have to finish this."

"I know," he answered quietly. "There is something really strange. When I leave here, I will be alone. But it is like you are never alone. Somehow it's like there is someone here with you in Tibet." His eyes narrowed, and for a moment he stared intently at me. "I think in some way you are doing this for your father."

I recoiled in surprise. Although I had spoken a lot about my family in general, I had never told Pascal anything about the recurring dream I had had since crossing the Lancang River—the dream in which I was riding a Tibetan pony across a landscape of ice, when a huge shadowy bird began pursuing us. Nor had I mentioned the poignant memories of hunting and other things that I hadn't thought about for years before we entered Tibet.

How was it that Pascal could look through my words and expressions to see and comprehend a part of me that was so well hidden, a part that even I didn't yet understand? I felt cold and vulnerable as I waited for him to use this knowledge to manipulate me into not finishing. Instead, he dug into his pack and handed me six rolls of film. I felt an almost tangible release.

"Well, I'm going," I said at last.

"Wade, take care coming back through those passes in December. There's going to be a lot of snow."

"I will."

I hugged him again, then stepped back. He looked old and tired. Loading on my pack, I turned and crossed through the prayer flags on either side of the pass. As I moved down the first set of steep switchbacks, I heard the zip of the motor drive on Pascal's F4 as he recorded my departure.

• • •

IT SEEMED AS though at any given time in Tibet I could hear bells. Sometimes it was the bells of Buddhist ceremonies, if there was a monastery nearby. More often it was the bells tied around the necks of livestock to help their owners locate the animals. Even when there seemed to be no one around, I could still hear bells. And so it was on my first night alone after leaving Pascal. All night long, through the thick veil of sleep, I thought I heard the tinkle of bells far off in the distance.

Snow fell during the night, but with little accumulation. By sunrise the storm had blown through. I awoke, carefully folded the plastic sheet, and packed my things. I ate soggy rice and leftover pork and eggs, then smashed the heavy steel can and buried it under a large rock. Just as I was getting ready to leave, I had the distinct feeling I was being watched. Turning slowly around, I found myself face to muzzle with a small brown mule. Around his neck was a large collar supporting a single copper bell, probably the source of the sound I had heard all night. I hadn't noticed the animal approach, so he must have walked very quietly.

"Well, hello," I said. "Where do you think you're going?" The little animal reared his head back at my words, producing a loud tinkling sound from his single bell. "You'd better head back the way you came. I'll bet someone is looking for you! Go on now, shoo!" I waved my arms and tried to startle the animal back up the trail, but to my surprise he would have none of it and instead tried to bolt past me. The trail was too narrow, though, and I was able to stop him. I hoisted my pack and started down the trail. The mule followed. Once again I stopped and tried to shoo him back up, but he stubbornly refused. "What is it with you?" I asked. The little animal walked steadily and purposefully on. I wondered, as we walked together, if this animal had a reason for wanting to leave. Maybe his owner was cruel, or maybe he was just sick of having to pack others' things day after day, eating when and what they decided, stopping for the night exactly where they wanted. Hey, I sympathized.

I decided it wasn't my business. After all, I wouldn't appreciate someone turning me in to the authorities. We walked on together. "You know, little brother," I said over my shoulder, "the price of freedom is that you have to find your own food now, and no one will be there to fix your feet when those shoes wear out—and remember, no more dry stables." The mule let out a snort and tried to get around me again. I moved out of the way and let him pass.

After a few hours the trail began to climb steeply up the side of the canyon. I was confused. There seemed to be no logical reason for it to go up here, as the canyon was still wide and inviting. I berated the trail builders under my breath and puffed up the steep incline. Soon I came upon the mule, munching hungrily at bamboo boughs that were hanging down from the hill above. "Better not hang out here too long; I'm sure they're on your trail." I passed him and moved on up the path.

After climbing fifteen hundred feet, during which time I thought up at least as many names for whoever had built the stinking road, I topped out at a small peak that was part of the ridge. For the first time since starting the trail, Kar-Kar-Po loomed into view, a massive hanging glacier making up most of its south face. The peak itself was lost in clouds. Here again were little stone houses made from the flat shale rocks that lay everywhere. I could see literally thousands of these little rock monuments, made by laying two flat rocks on edge and placing a larger flat rock over the top as a roof. Sometimes this was repeated to make a double-decker. Occasionally there was even a little notched-log ladder carved from a stick. The average height of the houses was about twenty inches. Inside these tiny structures were coins and paper money held down by rocks or, instead of money, tiny pieces of meat or butter. Beside these, rows of tsampa bowls were laid out in offering. Thousands of prayer flags tied on long bamboo poles fluttered in the wind, and many articles of clothing were hanging neatly on branches of trees or were simply strewn on the ground. A small path split off the trail and wandered through the trees and rocks for a hundred yards, rejoining itself near where it had left the main trail. There were so many clothes, hats, prayer flags, and other items hung on and above both sides that, as I walked through, I felt as if I were in a tunnel. Along the trail stone altars had been built, and in these had been left money and many different kinds of amulets. In one altar I counted over three hundred yuan, and it fascinated me that these people had enough respect for one another's faith that this money could just sit out here in the open and not be taken. The trail circled around a huge walnut tree whose branches were hung with all types of prayer beads, metal medallions, and little leather amulets and pouches, some with remarkably detailed craftsmanship. High up in the branches I caught the glint of metal, and when I climbed up several yards, I discovered an intricate medallion made of solid gold hanging from a leather thong. I took pictures with the camera Pascal had lent me, and eventually moved on.

The trail dropped steeply from there, following many switchbacks toward a torrent that roared off the massive glaciers of Kar-Kar-Po's south face. I had gone only a little way when I heard the sound of horse bells above. As I didn't want news of me to travel faster than I was, I started running down the trail looking for a place to hide. The steep mountainside was densely foliated, and it was difficult to get off the trail. Finally I came to a large walnut tree. I laid my pack beside the trunk, leaped up, and caught hold of the lower limbs, hauling myself high into the branches. Moments later the caravan thundered past below, eleven animals in all. A stockily built Tibetan wearing a sheepskin tunic, or *chubbas,* and a felt hat literally dragged the lead mule down the trail by its halter. A similarly dressed young boy, probably his son, brought up the rear with a bamboo whip-stick. The fourth animal in the caravan was the little brown mule I had walked with earlier that day.

"So, little brother. I guess the price was too great," I said under my breath.

ABOUT 2:00 P.M. I reached the bottom of the steep canyon and crossed the torrent on a cantilever bridge, arriving at a spacious open meadow surrounded by pine trees. Nine pilgrims, including the four women in blue caps whom I had seen earlier, rested in the tall grass. I got out my food and mixed tsampa with the tea they served me. They also gave me several strips of dried yak meat, which I ate hungrily. The other five pilgrims were a family: the father, whom I later learned was seventy-eight years old; his son, forty-five; and three daughters, the youngest in her late thirties and the oldest in her fifties. The son spoke simple Chinese and was kind to me. After we had eaten, he asked if I had medicine for his father, who was suffering from a stomachache. I adjusted him and gave him the last of some French antacid pills Sophi had given me when I was sick. After this the son told me that the youngest daughter was having back trouble from the heavy pack she was carrying, so I adjusted her too. The sound of the bones releasing scared her badly, and her brother had to hold her while I finished working, but afterward she reported feeling much better.

When the pilgrims packed their things, I decided to go with them and, if they didn't object, camp in the same place and share their fire. With only damp wood available, it would take me an hour and a half of constant effort to get a fire hot enough to burn on its own. The pilgrims had two of those primitive bellows made from the leg skin of a sheep or yak, so they could get a hot fire in ten minutes. To my dismay, the trail again began to climb up the side of the canyon. I realized that, being a sacred trail, it had to go to all the sacred spots, and in Tibet, these are usually at the tops of mountains.

As the evening wore on, it became apparent we would not reach the top before dark. For two hours we did not pass a spot where one person could sleep, let alone ten, and there was some talk of going back down to the river to camp. Just as it became dark, though, we came to a small cleft in the mountain and quickly set up camp. The women made a fire and cooked noodles. We all gathered wood for the fire and leaves to cushion against the wet earth. It looked like rain, so I set up a canopy over us with my plastic. After dinner I crawled into my sleeping bag beside the old man, who had taken a liking to me after I had soothed his stomachache. He rolled out a sheepskin beneath him, and over the top he put one wool blanket. I would have frozen with only that.

After everyone was bedded down, they began to sing. First the old man sang a song alone, then he started another in which he sang the first verse and the four women sang answering verses. For three hours straight they sang. One song about the Dalai Lama was very reverent and quiet. Of course I couldn't understand any of the words except "Dalai Lama." After singing, the pilgrims got onto their knees and said their evening prayers. Then they visited for a while, laughing and joking before finally going to sleep. In the morning when I questioned him, the old man's son told me all the songs had been religious.

ALL MORNING IT was up, up, up. Later when I looked at my maps, I determined we had climbed over forty-five hundred feet. It had rained during the night, so the trail was muddy and slippery, but the pilgrims pressed on doggedly, repeating their mantras. By this time it seemed I had been accepted as a fellow pilgrim, so the son took it upon himself to teach me proper pilgrim etiquette. Every time we came to a small puddle of water, each pilgrim took a bamboo branch, dipped it in, then flung water back over his shoulder. I was amazed at how much this ritual resembled a Catholic ceremony I had once seen, in which priests blessed the crowds with holy water. The pilgrims also counted on prayer beads that resembled Catholic rosaries. The next thing the son taught me was the mantra: *om mani padme hum ju, om mani padme hum ju*. This they repeated all day, at times just under their breath and at other times wailed in song at the top of their lungs. Late in the afternoon we reached the top of the mountain, where we came upon more of the little stone houses, some with money in them, others with offerings of butter or meat. Again the trail wound a rough circle around the top. The old man energetically prostrated himself on the ground, rose, and walked to the point where his hands had touched, then repeated this process. In this manner he laboriously traversed the rocky trail, and the others followed his example. It took almost half an hour for them to make it all the way around.

We dropped down again and eventually crossed the last pass before starting the torturous descent to the Nu River far below. Here the pilgrims again stopped to perform rites. They all faced Kar-Kar-Po, which at this time was directly north of us, and prostrated themselves many times. Next they got out large balls of wool and busily rushed around tying little strips to the trees, bushes, and shafts of prayer flags. I was also given a large ball of wool and some colored yarn. Finally they took the yarn and tied it to small angular stones, which they hung from a large tree where there were already many stones hanging. After this they continued down.

I stayed for a while and spent time comparing my maps to the country below. It was a clear day and I could see well into the mountains I would need to cross to get to the Drung valley. My topo maps were of a 1:500,000 scale, and this was one of the few times I was high enough and the weather clear enough to actually match them to the land and see specific features. For the hundredth time I was awed by the hugeness of this country.

I descended and soon caught up to the pilgrims, who had stopped to collect pitch splinters from the stump of a tree that had been cut last fall. Using my machete, I split out a large quantity for them and for myself. They burn like gasoline and are essential for starting fires in this humid climate. All Tibetan travelers carry a supply. Far below I could see a village perched on a ledge several hundred feet above the glacial torrent running off Kar-Kar-Po. It was built on the larger of two ledges jutting out from the crumbling canyon walls. These ledges were all that remained of the once smooth, rounded glacier-cut valley, now eroded by the river into a steep V-shaped gorge. This village wasn't on any of Pascal's maps, and although the pilgrim told me its name was Hopi, he knew little else about it.

We stopped for dinner above the village near a long row of water mills. There wasn't much flat ground so, after some discussion, the pilgrims decided to go into the village for the night. I didn't want to go there, but I knew that staying would arouse the suspicion of the pilgrims, who would probably tell the people of Hopi a foreigner was sleeping on the hill, so I followed them.

The pilgrims asked for a place to stay for the night, and we were shown to a large stable with high mud walls, half of which was covered by a roof. As always, many people showed up to look at me and my strange things. A burly man around thirty with blocky features and ragged Chinese clothes began arguing belligerently about me with the pilgrims. They spoke Tibetan, but I understood the names of the towns Bitu and Menkung. He held up three fingers, so I guessed he was talking about Pascal, Sophi, and me in our previous journey. He went on for quite some time, shaking his finger angrily at me while he spoke, and I started getting nervous. How had the word spread so far? Later a small Chinese man with a bad limp appeared and introduced himself, telling me he was a doctor. *"Dui dui, hao hao"* ("Yes yes, good good"), I answered in Chinese, then decided to pretend I couldn't speak much more than this in case it was to my advantage not to be able to understand what he said. He asked me what I was doing here and again

I answered, *"Dui dui, hao hao."* Undaunted by my lack of understanding, he continued to barrage me with questions. "What country are you from, France, America?" He asked in English, so I answered "England." I took out some money and said, *"Souyou,"* the Chinese word for Tibetan butter, indicating that I wanted to buy some.

The man led me to a house and inside introduced me to the village chief, a kind elderly man. The Chinese doctor and the chief had a long discussion about me while the wife of the house served fresh cornbread and a stew made of yak meat, turnips, and potatoes. The doctor could not speak Tibetan, so the only way he could communicate to the chief was through simple Chinese phrases, many of which I could understand. They talked about two other foreigners, Swedish botanists who had come through the mountains the previous year, and how they had been arrested, then sent away to Yunnan on horses. It was decided that I would spend the night here in the chief's house and in the morning someone would be sent to Trazo (the same village Sophi and Pascal had visited to get authorization to travel to Ridong) to fetch a policeman. I had no intention of going to Trazo. I ate and listened and ate more. The kindly old lady continued to fill my bowl and tea cup and push a bamboo basket filled with tiny loaves of bread toward me. I ate six bowls of soup and drank at least a quart and a half of butter tea.

After dinner the doctor took me from house to house to buy butter, but no one had any to sell at any price. As we walked through the dusty streets, I caught glimpses of the pilgrims scurrying about like mice, scrounging and pilfering odd sticks of firewood and begging for food. Eventually we returned to the stables, where the doctor gestured for me to pack my things and come with him. Instead I looked at him like he was crazy, took off my clothes, and crawled into my sleeping bag. He knelt down and shook my hand, saying he would see me in the morning, then left. The old pilgrim rose from where he was tending the cooking fire near the back wall of the stables and brought me some tea and food. I smiled my thanks. It made me sad to think that we would soon part. I drank the tea and put the food away for the next day.

I was exhausted, so when a crowd of young boys and girls gathered to gawk at me and touch my sleeping bag, I wanted to chase them off. One boy showed up with a handful of burning pine sticks like those I had cut earlier that day and held them over me so he could better examine me by the light of the flames. Terrified that a burning ember would fall on me, torching my sleeping bag or air mattress, I jumped up, swearing and gesticulating, not caring that I was dressed only in my underclothes. The crowd of young people laughed, and a couple of girls turned away in embarrassment. I crawled back into my sleeping bag and feigned sleep, hoping they would get bored with staring at me and go to bed. Instead, more people showed up. A little later a man started cranking on a fiddle. Oh crap! I thought. How rude to make so much noise while ten people who have hiked all day are trying to get some sleep. He stood not two yards away and tuned the noisy instrument. I suppressed a growing urge to jump up and mace him. Presently a second fiddler showed up. He joined with the first, and for a while they took off down the streets of the village. Suddenly I realized they were summoning people for a dance. "Arrgh!" I pulled my head under the covers and lay perfectly still. Why couldn't they dance somewhere else?

When the dance was in full swing, I looked at the pilgrims to see how they were tolerating this indignity. To my surprise they were all sitting up, big smiles lighting their faces. Obviously they were enjoying the activities. Gaiety, it seems, doesn't interfere with spirituality in the Buddhist religion. One of the fiddlers was a real comedian. He would sing the men's part so loudly his deep voice drowned out all the other men. Then suddenly, before the girls could sing their answering verse, he would jump in with a high squeaky female voice, at the same time making his fiddle sound high and squeaky, and sing their part. Everyone burst into laughter, including the pilgrims and, eventually, me. They had put on the dance for us. I would have loved to have gotten up and participated in the dance, but I was dog-tired and knew that tomorrow was going to be a marathon. It was October 28 and the moon was almost full. I watched through half-closed eyes as the circle of about forty young villagers danced in the light of the silver moon to the tune of the two fiddles.

AT 4:00 A.M. I roused my pilgrim friends, shaking each of them gently awake to say good-bye. "*Yamu, yamu*," they all said sadly as I squeezed their hands. They stared quietly at me from under their blankets as I put my sleeping bag away and shouldered the heavy pack.

As I hurried through the empty streets, a large, shaggy dog caught my scent and rushed out to terrorize me. I hurled a rock at the beast and continued to the edge of the village. The shrinking moon cast enough light that I could make out the way ahead, so I decided I could save the batteries of my headlamp. I walked quickly through the chill. A few hundred yards from the town, though, one of my feet caved through a soft spot on the shoulder, and I fell hard on the trail. It was about fifteen hundred feet straight down to the river, so I decided a little saved battery power wasn't worth the risk and switched the light back on. Hurrying down the trail, I felt some urgency, but at the same time felt calm inside. There was a chance, I knew, that the villagers might come after me in the morning, as they'd done in Ridong. But this time there was no hysterical captain to instigate a chase. I took the risk. This must be how a hunted animal feels, I thought, always having to run and hide, never quite knowing how much precaution is enough.

My father had often told me that to be a great hunter you had to be able to see things like an animal did, to actually get inside its skin and look out through its eyes. "This is the key to understanding people and animals," he said. He had raised as pets many of the same animals he hunted and had studied them closely.

"Think, Wade," he would quietly advise as we knelt at a set of tracks. "Where would you go from here if you were a bull elk walking through this forest?"

But though I was a crack shot and had become very good at other aspects of hunting at an early age, this ability to experience what another living creature did entirely escaped me. But it came, finally, in one day, in one instant.

Jackrabbits were everywhere, like great waves of gray water flowing over the smooth, rolling hills of eastern Idaho's portion of the Great Basin Desert. For the last seven years the population had been on the rise. That summer it had exploded, and as winter approached, bringing with it a scarcity of food, great herds of the starving animals swept over the farmland, devouring whole haystacks in their path.

The farmers fought back, erecting funnel-shaped holding pens where they could drive the hares in and club them to death. Shooting jackrabbits became a popular pastime.

My father and I had just arrived at the sight of a nuclear laboratory on the desert near Arco, Idaho. The instant we got out of the truck, there were jackrabbits everywhere. They came in waves over the low hills, and we began shooting immediately. I probably killed twenty in less than two minutes. At this time my back was still weak from my football injury, and it took some time after riding in the truck for my legs to loosen up enough for me to walk fast. After we annihilated the first wave of jacks, everyone spread out and started hiking ahead of me through the brush. I kept up the best I could, but soon they were out of sight over the first ridge, and I was alone. As I walked slowly on, I startled up a huge jackrabbit from the brush ahead. He was pure gray with only a few black marks on his tail and legs. He bounded ahead of me and stopped on a bare part of the hillside. Placing the crosshairs on his head, I squeezed the trigger, but just as I fired, he jumped. A small puff of fur flew from his back, and he fell on his side. I aimed at the head again to finish him off and squeezed the trigger. *Click*. I was out of bullets. I casually strode toward the hare, at the same time fishing in my pocket for more shells. The animal saw me coming and tried to get away, but his lower body was paralyzed, and he couldn't use his powerful hind legs. He frantically dug his front claws into the soft gray earth of the desert floor, trying to drag his body forward. The large brown eyes stretched wide with terror. I noticed that the bullet had only nicked the spine, knocking a groove out of the rabbit's back, and in the groove I could see the bony fragments of a shattered vertebra. All of this I watched with detached curiosity as I took out the twenty-five-round clip from my rifle and prepared to fill it. Then the hare began to scream. Anyone who has heard a wounded jackrabbit knows the sound is almost human.

It wasn't the first time I had heard it. I had wounded jacks before while hunting, and we even had a tape recording of an injured jackrabbit we used to call in coyotes. But this time it was different. I felt the pain in my own back, and in the struggling jack I could see myself, struggling for the past two years after my football injury, and I remembered my own feelings of helplessness. The rabbit screamed and screamed, and each time I wanted to open my mouth and scream with him. At the same time my hand fed a shell into the magazine of my rifle. There are some actions that, repeated so many times, can happen automatically, with no thought to them at all. I chambered the shell and fired the bullet. The jackrabbit instantly became silent and its body went stiff, vibrating with spasm. Its head arched back and the eyes stared widely at nothing. Bright red blood dribbled onto the ground. Gradually the body relaxed and went limp. I reached down and touched the warm body, feeling the supple lifelessness. I walked slowly back to the truck, where I put my .22 rifle in the front seat. I got in beside it and took out the empty magazine. After that I put away my guns forever.

Now, as I hiked through the darkness, I remembered the animal in Chyu I had seen being tortured by a young boy. I had just stepped into the street when my eyes fell upon a small crowd of people gathered around a young boy torturing a rabbit. He held the poor creature up by a length of wire twisted around its neck, then brought back a tiny stick and smacked it across its back. The crowd of people laughed and I felt myself moving toward the boy. "No, Wade!" Pascal leaped in front of me. "This is not your affair!" I tried to shove past him, but he grabbed one of my wrists. "Please, it is just a rat. Don't make trouble from this!" I looked again and Pascal was right, what was hanging from the wire by its grotesque pink tail was a large gray rat, not a rabbit at all. The young boy stared at me in apprehension for a few seconds, then went back to his gruesome play, this time slowly pushing the shrieking creature's head into one of the sewer canals that ran open on both sides of the street. I shook loose from Pascal and hurried down the street toward the police station.

"Really, Wade, you are too sensitive, you are really crazy sometimes," Pascal said. A vision of thousands of rabbits bounding across the plateau had crept into my mind, but I had pushed it away. Now I was the one being hunted, and the image of the fleeing jackrabbits had come back to me.

IN ROUGHLY THREE hours I reached the Nu River, where the huge Lakonra lamasery, now deserted, stood guarding the trail. The path here was chiseled into solid stone, and long piles of carved mantra-rocks split the trail at regular intervals. The walls of the canyon for as high as I could reach were engraved with Tibetan script and many Buddhist figures. A trail cut back north upriver, but none continued south, the direction I needed to travel. There was, however, a trail on the opposite side of the river, and I wondered if I had to first go north to a bridge, then cross and come downstream. I hid my pack and then backtracked up the trail I had just come down. Eventually I found where I had missed the fork, retrieved my pack, and headed downstream on the east side. Soon the trail on the opposite side of the river vanished among some high cliffs, so again I had made the right choice.

I hiked steadily downstream for five hours, eating packs of uncooked ramen noodles to keep up my energy. I never would have gotten Pascal to do this. I wanted to be sure I wouldn't be stopped this time before reaching the Drung valley. At a deep bend in the river, I passed a Tibetan man with several mules. His eyes bugged out in surprise when he saw me, and he refused the cigarette I offered. I recognized him as a villager from Menkung. "Where are the other two?" he demanded shakily. I told him I didn't know what he was talking about, hoping he would think he had mistaken me. "You know! The girl and the other man with the beard! Weren't you arrested by the police?" he asked suspiciously, locking his wrists together to indicate handcuffs. I tried to look bewildered at what he was saying. "Are you still trying to reach the Drung River?" he asked, using the official Chinese word, "Dulong." I told him no, I was headed to Gongshan in Yunnan. I could tell he didn't believe me. I asked if there was a bridge ahead and he said the nearest was three days away, but in a couple of hours I would reach a cable crossing belonging to a village, Zhaen, on the opposite side. He named all the other villages from here to the bridge, but none of them sounded remotely like the ones on Pascal's map. By the time I reached the cable crossing, I was beat. I built a small fire and fixed noodles and hot milk from powder.

All over Tibet and China single-cable bridges, each made with an inch-and-a-quarter-diameter cable, slope across rivers, a line heading in each direction. To cross, villagers put a wooden block over the cable and a loop of hemp to sit in—and *whee*! After eating I rigged my ice ax and two carabiners in such a way that I could use them to send my pack sliding across the cable. Unfortunately, this would leave with no way to slide across myself. I wondered if I was strong enough to hand-over-hand the two hundred yards of thick cable or if I should just try to swim the river.

As I was deliberating, a young man of about nineteen came along the trail with a large bamboo basket strapped to his back. He was very tiny and had pointed features, and I realized that he couldn't possibly be Tibetan or Chinese. He spoke no Chinese, but when I showed him with gestures that I wanted to cross the river, without hesitating he stuffed his basket into a nearby clump of grass and pulled out the long cotton strap he had used to tie it to his back. Near the cables he retrieved a block of hardwood with a groove cut into it and a long strap of leather. Fitting the block of wood over the cable, he wrapped the leather strap over it and tied the strap around his waist, then used the frayed cotton strap to tie my backpack to himself. Fearing the strap would break and my pack might be lost, I quickly took out the camera bag. Last of all he pulled from his pocket a glass bottle filled with water, which had a few twigs stuffed in the top to slow the flow. Upending the bottle of water to wet the cable ahead of him, he let go and shot out across the Nu River at tremendous speed. In less than a minute he was at the other side, climbing down to refill the water bottle. He then climbed up to the second cable and, within a minute, came whistling back. Now it was my turn. I realized suddenly that he was going to use that same frayed cotton strap for me! I had thought he would just let me use his rig, but he must have felt I was too inexperienced to go alone. It was some small relief that he doubled the strap. I did some quick mental calculations. My pack weighed around eighty-five pounds, double that would be a hundred and seventy. I usually weighed a hundred and seventy-five, but had probably lost at least five pounds, so it should hold. Then *wheeeeee*, we were off! For an instant it was sheer beauty to be moving at such an incredible speed over the open water. Then somehow we got off balance and kinked the block of wood sideways, which brought us to a grinding halt about thirty yards from the opposite side. After we got ourselves straightened out, the small man took some water into his mouth and spit it out onto the cable in front of us, then tried vainly to haul us the rest of the way across. The last section of the cable turned upward to keep the person crossing from smashing into the opposite side, and he was not strong enough to pull us both up this incline. I tried to help, but because of the difference in our weight, when I turned sideways to pull, it kinked the system and we still couldn't move. Suddenly we both cracked up laughing. I looked across the cable at the little man, whose elfin features were twisted in mirth. Then he saw something and yelled at the opposite shore. I looked and saw several people standing there. They all got hold of the cable, and their combined weight flexed it down so we slid easily the rest of the way across.

I gave the man a pack of cigarettes. A very stern Tibetan man was among our rescuers. He questioned me thoroughly in poor Chinese and roughly went through the contents of my pack without asking. Eventually he became a little more friendly and, when another man came across the cable with a muzzle-loading rifle and a large basket of oranges, the stern man told me to go with this new arrival to the village. The man who had taken me across the cable and the rest of the villagers who had gathered all crossed back over and headed into the fields above the main trail.

I followed the Tibetan man with the rifle up to the village, about a thirty-minute walk from the cable crossing. It was an enchanting place. The houses were built right into gray, limestone cliffs that towered on all sides. This close to the river, the area was still a desert environment, and cacti grew in abundance. It was like a living, breathing Mesa Verde. We entered the man's house, and his sister and mother cooked me a large dinner of buckwheat bread and pork with, of course, lots of butter tea. The man spoke reasonably good Chinese. He was very nice but high-strung and fidgety. At first he didn't trust me and inquired suspiciously about where I was going. "Are you one of those three who want to get to the Drung River?

"No," I lied, "I'm going to the big white snowy mountains north of the village."

"Those three were bad people," he continued. "They didn't have a paper from the Gongchandang [Communist Party]." He stamped his hand in the way that I had learned meant official document. "They got arrested!" He crossed his wrist to indicate handcuffs, just as the other man had earlier that day, and I felt a shiver as I remembered the cold steel clamped so tightly on my wrist.

After eating, the man showed me a severely abscessed carbuncle on his left arm. I lanced and cleaned it, then gave him some antibiotic ointment. He also had a headache, so I checked his spine and adjusted his atlas vertebra. Other villagers came by and asked if I had medicine for dysentery, the most common ailment here. I had very little left.

The family invited me to spend the night. I was tired,

but I also wanted to get away from the Nu River and into the mountains in case there was trouble. It seemed that everyone knew of Pascal, Sophi, and me, and I had no idea how quickly the authorities would react once they figured out that one of us was back.

The man's sister gave me a giant round loaf of buckwheat bread, which I put into the top of my pack. I thanked her, and we left the house. The man led me to where there was a fork in the trail leaving the village. "If you want to go to those big white mountains, you go this way." He indicated a steep trail winding up the side of the gorge. "But if you're trying to reach the Drung River, this is the path," he said, pointing out a thin trail that followed the river through the gorge. "Follow this river until there is no more water, then cross two mountains. *Yamu, yamu,*" he said, and we parted. He had known all along that I was lying.

I felt dirty as I walked away. I suddenly saw myself as I imagined they must see me—a selfish Westerner, coming suddenly into their quiet lives, then disappearing, leaving trouble behind and them to pick up the pieces. Why, I wondered, was it so important to be first to this obscure place, when these people were struggling under terrible conditions and a repressive government. Being first! Winning! That was what it was all about.

To be number one, just like high school football. That was the only reason Pascal had been able to lure me back to China. But now I wasn't so sure it was enough. On both of my trips with Pascal into these forbidden areas, we had upset the lives of the people we met. That's what had troubled Sophi so deeply, and I guess on some level the realization had been growing in me. But I had brushed these thoughts aside, blaming Pascal, without acknowledging my own part in it. Now I was alone, and what did I do? Just what Pascal would have done: lie, bluff, evade. I had to admit part of me liked it when Pascal teased and razzed the Chinese officials. They were asking for it, I felt. Maybe it was their authority, their attempt to control everything. In any case, I found myself looking at them much the same as my father had taught me to think of game wardens and traffic cops—as a kind of evil. But though it might embarrass a fish-and-game officer back home if I eluded him with a backpack full of venison, here we could cost these military and police officials their careers, which put the people who helped us, people over whom the officials had authority, in real danger. I wasn't sure if it was justifiable. Certainly it seemed wrong to lie to and endanger the villagers who freely shared food and helped us in so many ways.

FOR THREE HOURS, I climbed up the trail, crossing back and forth over the river on cantilever bridges. Just as it was getting dark I reached a small shanty with smoke coming through the roof. Inside were an old man and woman cooking dinner over an open fire. They showed only mild surprise at my arrival and took me right in for tea and food. I shared my buckwheat bread, and they cooked me several ears of corn. Neither could speak any Chinese, but they jabbered away in Tibetan, seeming to care not at all that I couldn't respond. We laughed together and ate. The old woman snorted snuff from a small silver box, while the man smoked tobacco in a long pipe with a brass bowl. They had one cooking pot, one tea kettle, a leather bag full of butter, and another with tsampa. Besides these, I could discover no other implements or supplies in the hut. Their beds were made of rough-hewn boards propped up on rocks and covered with buckwheat straw. After eating, the woman combed my hair with a large wooden comb she produced from the folds of her cloak, and the man made me a bed of buckwheat straw under an extension of the roof of the shanty. I slept for twelve hours. In the morning I was stiff and sore but eager to get on my way.

After I'd hiked for a few hours, the creek forked and the trail ended at a group of deserted summer shanties. There was no one to ask where to go, and I couldn't get a clear idea from my maps. I spied a plume of smoke high up on the side of the mountains, so I hid my pack and climbed up to a small valley, where I found about ten people living in two large houses. They were small with fine features, like the young man who had taken me across the cable, and I realized they must be Drung or some other minority. Certainly they were not Tibetan. They seemed shocked to see me. No one smiled, and none of them could speak Chinese. Through gestures I indicated that I wanted to cross the mountains, and one man pointed up the left fork of the canyon. I thanked him the best I could and started back down. On the trail to the river, I met another man carrying a bamboo basket full of corn. When I again gestured that I wanted to cross the mountains, he confirmed that I was to go up the left fork. He then took both of my hands and held them up so there was a notch between the thumb and the fingers, then traced a trail through my hands, indicating that I was to go through two passes (or so it seemed to me). He did this twice, then picked up his load and continued on.

As dusk approached, I found myself on a small trail, on a narrow, steep ridge that fell vertically on both sides to roaring streams below. With only half an hour of light left,

I knew I had to do something about finding a campsite. Leaving the ridge, I bushwhacked my way through the bamboo down the steep embankment. Finally, I reached the stream, but the bank dropped right into the creek. Discouraged, I chopped my way up the stream about fifty yards, eventually coming to a small landslide. An upturned boulder formed a platform, which I was able to improve by crib-walling rocks beside it. I cut a lot of bamboo to put between my sleeping gear and the mud. By the time I was ready to make the fire, it was already dark, and I still had to build another small platform for the fire to burn on. Everything was soaking wet and muddy. Normally under these conditions it would have taken two hours to get a fire hot enough to boil water, but I took out a small foil package of Sterno I had carried for this kind of emergency and soon had a smoky blaze going from dead bamboo. After a meal of noodles and canned ham, I crawled into my sleeping bag, my feet hanging out into space from the platform. It was very discouraging. Then, as clear as if he were standing beside me, I heard my father's voice. *You just have to stick out the tough times.* Soon, in spite of the uncomfortable bed, I slept, and for the last time I dreamed the two dreams that had started that first night after crossing the Lancang River—of hunting the buck, and of being pursued by a great black bird.

NINE

The Drung

I WOKE UP cold. Everything was frozen. I shook the ice off my now almost useless sleeping bag and quickly packed. I bushwhacked back up to the ridge, using my ice ax to hook trees ahead and pull myself up the steep, muddy incline, keeping the machete in the other hand to cut the bamboo that got hung up in my pack. It was arduous, but I was glad to finally get out. My mind was unnaturally clear. I moved slowly and rested often. At the tree line I stopped and built a fire to cook some noodles. Ahead the pass was looming into view, and new snow glittered in the morning sun. I finished eating, hoisted my pack, and started up again. Then I stopped. Billowing dark clouds were suddenly visible on the tops of the mountains. *Cumulonimbus clouds, storm clouds,* came the voice of my father for a second time. Then: *There's no high stria, and they're moving pretty fast. Probably won't do much more than spit on us.* Again I was struck by the strangeness of hearing my father's voice in my mind. I moved on, climbing slowly up the steep valley toward the pass.

I knew from my maps that the pass was around 15,000 feet. It took tremendous effort for me to move forward with such a heavy pack at this altitude. My mind remained clear, though, and silent. Hours later I reached the pass, exhausted, but something looked terribly wrong on the other side. The valley I stared into resembled nothing on my topo map and there were few trees, and those few were lower than where I thought they should be.

I photographed the country, then started down. After descending three thousand feet, my legs rubbery, I began to encounter marshlands and realized this entire valley was seeping with springs. There was absolutely no place to set up camp, and it was already late afternoon. I decided I would have to head downstream until I found something better. I slogged along for several hundred yards when, just as clearly as the other two times, my father's voice came to me. *Us locals usually know what we're talking about.* I stopped, stunned that I had forgotten that the villagers had told me to go through two passes. I looked up, but could see neither the pass I had come through nor any sign of another pass. "Dad, I don't know where it is," I said aloud. There was no answer. Had I actually expected one?

"DIVE RIGHT, PASS left on two, break!"

For fifteen years my father had coached the Camas County football team in Fairfield, Idaho. A great athlete himself, he had demanded excellence from his players, driving them with his unending energy and somehow infusing in simple farm kids a burning desire to be the best. Season after season he had led them to victory, and year after year the yells of triumph had echoed from the pep assemblies in the old brick gym and down the halls, past glass-front shelves crowded with trophies. Once his sons had gotten old enough to play, he had quit. From then on he watched from the sidelines.

I vividly remember exploding from the line that day, driven forward by a rage that had been a part of me even then—a rage all the hotter for wanting to be something great and instead finding myself a mediocre end on a losing team. But more than that, it was rage at the game itself. I hated football with every fiber of my being.

That day I ran for all I was worth, five, ten, twenty yards, cut hard to the left, and looked back. The other receiver was covered by two safeties and the defense was crashing through our line, closing in on our quarterback for the third straight play. He danced around frantically, then hurled the ball in my direction. The instant he released it I knew it was too high. He was simply getting rid of it so he wouldn't get mangled again and lose yardage. I sprinted as fast as I could to try to get far enough downfield so I could reach the ball, to bring it down into my arms. The ball appeared directly overhead. I jumped, stretching my body as high as possible. My fingers touched the dark brown leather and then there was a terrible impact.

Like the huge buck I'd shot the year before, I felt myself twisting in the air; then I landed with a thud on my belly. Slowly I opened my eyes and saw two white legs in front of my face. At first I thought they were my own, but it was the boy who had speared me, a safety who had button-hooked then smashed into me, using his head as a battering ram. A few yards from him a yellow penalty flag lay crumpled in the grass. Something was terribly wrong with the lower part of my body. I pulled my arms under me and started to push myself up. Unbelievable pain shot from my low back to the bottoms of my heels on both feet. Nothing had ever hurt so much in my entire life. I saw my father watching from the sidelines, the sidelines from which he had watched every game I had ever played, always shouting above the roar of the crowd. But now he was quiet and his face expressionless. Through the searing pain it occurred to me that he was waiting for me to get up, that he really had no idea yet how badly I was hurting.

I spent nearly four months in a body cast. My football days were over, and I eventually dropped out of high school too. It was three years before I could walk again without pain.

I STARTED UP the side of the valley, hoping the pass would become visible as I traveled higher. My legs were still rubbery, and when I looked down, my hands were shaking. "Dad," I called out again. "Dad, I can't do it. I'm too tired."

You'd better eat something, son. You can't expect to run on empty for very long.

I stopped and pulled out a Power Bar. I ate it along with a few mouthfuls of tsampa and some powdered milk, washing it all down with water from my canteen.

Have butter, Wade. Lots of good calories in butter.

Even in my extended state, my mind remained sharp and clear. I puzzled over the strange, disjointed sentences from my father. I knew that people had altered states of mind at high altitudes, especially during extreme exertion, but I had many times been a lot higher than this and nothing like this had ever happened to me.

The clouds grew thicker above me, and again my father's voice spoke. *Looks like we are in for a little weather. Son, put on a jacket before you go out. You'll freeze to death in just that sweatshirt.* With this last sentence an image of myself—an eleven-year-old boy, a single-shot twenty-gauge clutched in one hand, a canvas bag of shells in the other—flashed to my mind. I was standing in the door of my parents' house, and there, towering over me, stood my father dressed in his thick down coat, the fur earflaps of his hunting cap turned up. Beside him, propped against the wall, was his over-and-under Savage twelve-gauge shotgun and a thermos of coffee. He handed a blue coat to the young boy. Dutifully I leaned the gun against the wall and pulled on the jacket. The image faded, and it was then that I understood. The voices I was hearing were not something I was generating in my mind. They were memories, memories from my childhood, small incidents perfectly recorded somewhere, but then entirely forgotten.

Somehow, through the intense physical exertion, cold, and depravation, my mind had become clear. The rippling, splashing cascade of dialogue and images from everyday thought was entirely absent. Snow began to swirl down from the clouds above, but it was really too cold to snow; the flakes were more like ice crystals. I pulled on my last layer of warm clothes and continued up. The voice of my father spoke more and more frequently now, and with it came memories of my childhood long forgotten yet so vivid in detail they could have happened just moments before. *Come on, just ten more reps*: my father's encouraging voice as I cranked out my last set of bench presses in the small weight gym above the high school basketball court. Snow swirled around my feet. I counted ten more steps up the mountain, then stopped. My breath came in deep, ragged gasps in the thin air. I leaned on my ice ax—I was leaning on my hunting rifle, both hands clamped tightly about the barrel, the butt resting in the new snow. I felt that my small lungs were going to burst with exertion. *Come on. Let's get to those rocks. You can rest there while I set up the coyote call*. I watched him trudge forward to the small outcropping of rocks. He was dressed all in white, a rifle slung over one shoulder, a shotgun over the other. There was a full moon, and we were going to try to call in some coyotes.

I dug in my ice ax and followed him. The black cloud loomed above me, and I looked up. Somehow it seemed to resemble a huge black bird, wings stretched out above the mountains—like the bird from my dream. *That dirty son of a gun!* A raven. It had risen higher in the sky, the whites of an egg visible in its beak. Two meadowlarks were hot in pursuit. Dad stomped the gas pedal of the old Toyota Corona to the floor, speed-shifting into third gear. I watched the speedometer climb. The raven was just crossing the road above us. *Here! Take the wheel!* He leaned back, reaching into the seat behind, and snatched up the Browning twelve-gauge. The raven suddenly veered into my field of vision, above and in front of the car. There was a muffled report as the sound of the shotgun came through the roof of the car. A cloud of black feathers burst from the bird and it folded, falling like a stone into a freshly plowed field. Dad pulled the gun back into the car and laid it between us. His face was lit with the glow of absolute triumph. *Hell of a shot, huh?* I looked back into the sky and the black cloud had changed shape. It no longer resembled a bird, or anything else.

The pass was just ahead. I walked forward—I ran. The old red Chevy pickup stood in the driveway, and through the window of the camper I could see fishing poles and sleeping bags. I missed him so. *Hell of a shot, son.* We both stood over the big five-point buck, and I felt a pride long forgotten well up in my chest. It was a beautiful autumn day, not a cloud in the sky. I could smell the buck brush, the musk of the deer, and freshly cut pine wood from my father's clothes. I ran on.

"Daddy, it's been four days!" He stepped out of the truck, reached down, scooped me up, and hoisted me high over his head with one arm. It was his favorite trick. *If you get much bigger, I won't be able to do that anymore.*

This last memory flickered in my mind, dimmed, and was gone. I stood at the pass and stared down into the steep, heavily treed canyons of the Drung valley far below. It was still snowing lightly, but beyond the clouds to the west was some blue sky. I remembered Pascal's words right before we parted: *Somehow it's like there is someone here with you in Tibet. I think in some way you are doing this for your father.* At the time this had seemed crazy, because my father hadn't even approved of this trip. How could I be doing anything *for* him by coming here? And why here in Tibet?

My breathing was loud, even in my own ears. It was automatic, and I felt almost detached from my physical body, which was numb with cold. I took pictures, then started down. There was no trail, so I assumed the locals rarely came through here. I knew I was physically exhausted. The wind was freezing. I descended into a steep V-shaped valley that rapidly became steeper the further down I went. Shortly I came to a vertical section that required rock climbing. I took off my pack and carefully down-climbed, tapping holes with the adze of my ice ax to make sure the rock was solid. Then I climbed back up, retrieved the pack, and started down again. It was 7:00 P.M. and the sun was almost gone.

Technically, the climbing wasn't particularly difficult, but I was exhausted, and a fall here could easily have been fatal. Skiffs of new snow plastered the rocks and the sparse tufts of wiry grass, making the otherwise easy ground below the cliffs treacherously slick. In an unguarded moment my left foot shot out from under me, and I pitched sideways down the slope, driven forward by the heavy pack. My chest slammed hard against a rock and I began sliding rapidly backward on my side toward the next ragged cliff band. With all my strength I dragged the ice ax under me in the self-arrest maneuver, instinctively digging the pick into the frozen rocky sod, which brought me to a grinding stop. Rolling the rest of the way onto my belly, I dug in my boots and stood, then turned slowly and looked down at the jagged rocky ledges that would have broken my fall and my body had I kept sliding. I felt a fleeting, weak burst of adrenaline; then again I was numb.

It was well after dark when I finally reached a series of small, sloping ledges, beyond which the stream plummeted over a precipice. Even though I knew I was only a few hundred feet below the pass, there was no chance of going down farther that night. Working frantically, I built a small bivouac shelter using the plastic sheet and lots of rocks. Nearby I found dry fuel in the form of dead brush and soon had a smoky fire going in the protection of a corner of the platform I was on. I ate noodles and ham again, and had a cup of hot milk. Working laboriously by headlamp, I kneaded and fluffed the frozen sleeping bag until some of the loft, which is essential to warmth, returned. Wearing all my clothes, I crawled under the plastic and into the bag. Outside the wind raged down off the glaciers from the mountain above, pelting my shelter with snow crystals, but inside I was warm, and in spite of the howling of the storm, rapidly fell into a deep, dreamless sleep.

When I awoke, it was sunny and clear, and the ordeal

of the night before seemed like a fading memory. I unzipped the sleeping bag and gingerly explored a deep-purple bruise across my left lower rib cage. With a jolt I felt the sudden fear of tumbling toward the cliff—an emotional response I had been too tired to experience at the time it had happened. I closed my eyes and slept again.

In the late afternoon the clouds formed again and it began to snow lightly. I pulled myself stiffly from the shelter and brushed the snow from the fire ring I had built the night before. There was little wood left, and what I found wasn't good, but after three hours of blowing and fanning I had a fire hot enough to boil water for the evening meal— my only meal that day. Around 6:00 P.M. I crawled back into my sleeping bag and slept until the next morning.

SO TODAY WAS the day! The first of November, the day I would finally get to meet the Drung people. I munched some ramen noodles cold, then spent a little time catching up my journal. With a day's rest, I felt some of my old enthusiasm return. "What would these people be like?" I wrote. "Would they feed me or would they be afraid and try to hurt me?" If Pascal's information was right, I would be the first Westerner they had ever seen. I wondered if this would actually prove to be true. Well, if worst came to worst, I still had enough freeze-dried food left to get back over the mountains in good shape.

The temperature had dropped below freezing again during the night. Thick frost coated everything, and I couldn't believe how cold it was up here compared to the valleys below. I'll be there soon enough, I thought, as I shook the ice from my plastic tarp and started to pack,

making a mental note that I had begun the malaria pro-
phylactic medicine on that day, a Tuesday.

Midmorning I started down. After a short way, the
canyon became even more narrow and steep, and eventually I came to a cliff with a small stream cascading over a
forty-five-foot waterfall. It was far too difficult to negotiate
with the pack, so first I lowered it to the ledge below with
the light plastic cord I had brought for making shelters,
then down-climbed to it. A short distance later I came to
another cliff and again lowered the pack and climbed after
it. This time the down-climbing was more difficult, and it
took a long time to figure out the moves. I longed for the
8mm climbing rope we had bought in Hong Kong, but I
had sent it out with Sophi.

The canyon was a deep V, through which rushed the tiny
stream. Often there was no room to walk along the sides and
I was forced to walk down the stream itself. The rocks in and
around the water were covered by a thin film of ice condensed
from the misty spray flung off the gushing water, and each
time it was necessary to cross, I slipped and stumbled like a
drunkard, banging my ankles and feet and occasionally
falling into the water. I was bruised, wet, cold, and miserable.

Eventually the canyon again cliffed out, and the rock
was dead vertical with almost no features. This time, after
lowering the pack, I had to traverse far out onto the canyon
wall, following a system of horizontal cracks in the rotten
limestone until I came to a place where the angle of the
rocks lessened, and again I was able to climb down to my
pack. My Teva sandals had sticky rock-climbing rubber on
the soles, but even with that, the climbing was far more difficult than I felt safe doing unroped.

Leaving the heavy pack, I crawled down to the next cliff, where I cautiously made my way out to the edge of an icy lip of worn limestone. The tiny stream rocketed over and fell free for eighty feet to a rippling blue pool at the bottom. There was no possible way to continue down there. I would have to retreat and try to climb out of the canyon. I laboriously worked my way back up the cliff I had just descended, then dragged the pack up behind me. Here the canyon wall was clay and mud, and not quite as steep as in other places. I first attempted to climb up the slippery incline, digging in my feet and pulling on vegetation that jutted out from the wall. With tremendous effort I got ten feet up, then one of the bushes pulled free and I slid back down the oozing bank into the stream from which I had started. On the second attempt I made it less than half as far before again pulling loose and sliding back into the water. I was trapped!

Frightened and frantic, I searched for another possibility. If I couldn't get out here, I would be forced to go upstream all the way to the head of the canyon, which was far above the tree line and at least half a day's journey. Finally I returned to the shallow, rotten cracks I had descended earlier. There might be a possible route through a band of horizontal rock layers, above. Taking a deep breath to calm myself, I carefully traversed out again and began tediously chipping steps and holes up the steep wall of loose shale rock. An hour later I reached the top, where the thick floor of the jungle hung over the eroded sides of the canyon like ragged edges of an immense carpet. Beneath was a crumbly vertical wall of topsoil and humus. I gingerly traversed several yards left, to where a gnarled tree root protruded from the crumbling dirt. It proved solid and I was able to haul myself up onto it, then stand and reach the trunk of the tree from which it grew. I crawled up into the forest and hugged the trees in relief, then cautiously hauled the pack up behind me. Had the thin cord broken, the pack would have been lost, as I could not have brought myself to attempt climbing back down into the canyon again.

Now that I was in the forest, a new nightmare began. The bamboo stalks were tiny and flexible and grew so close together that I could go only two or three steps, with tremendous effort, before being bound up and stopped altogether. I took out the machete and cut what was holding me back, then went on for two or three more steps, only to be stopped again. After another hour I had traveled less than fifty yards up and was exhausted. I ate another package of raw noodles and drank the last of my water, then trudged on, realizing that if things didn't improve, it would be several days before I reached the valley below.

Again I felt discouragement gnawing at my willpower, and my rests became longer and closer together. I was getting thirsty too, and the only water I knew of was far below in the canyon out of which I had just crawled. In my anxiety to get out, I had not thought to fill my two canteens before climbing up.

Then, during a rest, I suddenly realized I had come to a trail. It was hardly one at all, just a few little dents in the earth winding across the side hill with the worst of the bamboo broken back. In fact, because I had pushed the bamboo down ahead of me, I had covered it up and almost passed right over and missed it. Words can't describe the relief I felt at finally being able to move at a decent pace again. Suddenly the forest was beautiful. For the first time since I had descended from the passes, I was able to enjoy the beauty of what was around me, the wildlife, the monkeys playing in the trees and the many kinds of birds.

Late in the evening I arrived at the banks of the Nabalo River, a large tributary to the Irrawaddy. The trail had petered out several miles before in the jumbled remains of an avalanche, and I followed a dry streambed the rest of the way. To my surprise, there was absolutely no sign of people anywhere: no footprints, no wood cuttings, no trails. All my energy had been focused on reaching the Drung valley, and it had never occurred to me that, the moment I arrived, there wouldn't be people. But this was virgin forest, and if people were here, they were certainly well hidden. I set up camp on a flat, dry sandbar, built a large fire, and cooked dinner. I stayed up late drying my sleeping bag, shoes, and clothes, which had become soaked during my bushwhack through the bamboo forest. "Never," I resolved, "will I bring a down bag to such a humid place again."

I ALLOWED MYSELF a big breakfast the next morning, a large pan of noodles with the last of my yak butter. I shook out my sleeping bag, which was so stiff with ice I had trouble packing it into its stuff sack. For hours I trudged through the forest. Sometimes I found small game trails, and other times there was nothing, and still there was no sign whatsoever of people. In places the foliage was so high and thick I was forced again to cut my way through with the machete, but as long as I could stay under the trees, the smaller foliage wasn't too thick. The rain forest was a mixture of deciduous trees and huge conifers. Thick moss grew over everything, and deeply veined dark-green ferns wound their way up the trunks of the trees. The soft forest floor, a carpet of pine needles, moss, and decaying wood, completely silenced my footsteps.

Early in the afternoon, near the river, I found a single, bare human footprint. It was the first sign of people since the prayer flags in the second pass I had crossed three days earlier. I was reminded of Robinson Crusoe, and probably just as excited as he was when he found Friday's footprints. A little later I picked up a trail along which there were woodcuttings and occasionally the remains of a campfire. The bamboo had been cut back at an angle and afterward had grown back up. There were places where I had to be extremely careful not to trip and fall or I would be impaled. The trail wound along the river's edge, following the path of least resistance. At streams it went up or down until it came to the first natural tree crossing. There was no effort at maintenance, and at times I lost the trail altogether and was again forced to cut my way through the thick undergrowth.

In the late afternoon the valley widened, and the trail became much better. Steep inclines were fitted with notched-log ladders, much like in Tibet, and the worst of the logs were cut out of the way. There were more and more footprints, and from these, I began to know a little about the people I had come to meet. They were tiny. Their small feet sank into the soft earth only half as far as mine, and the print was deeper at the toe, indicating that they were moving quickly and nimbly. I hurried on, excited to meet these people who until now had been just a concept: "the Drung People."

Eventually I started passing cornfields, all strangely deserted although in various stages of harvest and cultivation. In some places I found stacks of firewood, and although I found wood chippings in the mud that could have been no more than an hour old, there were no people. Where in the world were they?

The first indication that they were hiding from me came when I rounded a small bend in the stream just in time to see a tiny head disappear in the cornfield on the hill above. Could I really be that frightening to these people? I asked myself.

The trail climbed higher up the side of a canyon dense with foliage before emerging again at a pass from where I could see a village in the widening valley. Like the people, the houses were very small—square log structures with thatched roofs, through which smoke rose lazily. Trails connecting the houses had short rock walls on either side, and a mist rose from the cornfields and forest on both sides of the river. The whole scene looked like something out of a fairy tale, and I would not have been greatly shocked if seven dwarfs had come marching up the trail, whistling as they went! But again, I could see no one.

I descended into the valley and followed the trail until I came to the first of the houses. Smoke rose through the roof and there was bedding hanging from a line, but no people. I circled slowly around the building, taking in my first view of a Drung home. Above the door hung two crossbows, and a little over from them were tacked some monkey hides, flesh side out. The logs were poorly fitted, but there was no chinking. The poles for the roof, the thatching, and even a small rail that ran around the front porch were all cleverly fitted together with notching and grooves and forked sticks, then bound tightly with jute. No nails. At the side of the house was a tiny square window without shutters or closures of any kind, and there was one of these at the back of the house too.

I continued around to the opposite side of the building, and here I met my first Drung. Crouched down between the house and a low stone wall, obviously hiding, she was so tiny that at first I thought she was a child. Her back was to me as she peered intently around the corner to the front of the house, which I had just left. Suddenly she turned full about, eyes wide, and for an instant regarded me with a gaze of pure terror. She was an old lady. Wrapped around her body was a strange, one-piece length of cloth, and her face was grotesquely tattooed, especially around the mouth. Perched upon her head was a tiny pointed hat made of gray cloth, held on by straps under her chin. In the next instant she let out a yelp, jumped up, and fled down the trail toward the village, her dog following.

I came slowly behind, wondering what I should do now. I had not anticipated that my first encounter with these people would actually be of such a traumatic nature, and I felt some apprehension about what would happen next. Would they, as Pascal had assured me once I'd resolved to push on alone, come out and shoot me full of poison darts from their crossbows? Or would the whole village pack up their valuables and hide in the mountains, as had happened in the lower Drung valley when a Chinese journalist had visited several years ago?

I sat down and waited for half an hour before going on into the village so the people would have time to settle down. No one came out to see me. Finally I got up, shouldered my pack, and slowly walked toward the village. I waited for the *twang* of a crossbow or the screams of terror as the villagers fled before me into the mountains. I thought I was prepared for anything, and yet what happened next again took me fully by surprise.

A tiny Drung man wearing a new checkered sports coat and clean slacks stepped out from behind the first building in front of me and, in fluent Chinese, demanded to know what I was doing. I stopped, stammered for a moment, and then told him I had just come down from Tibet and was looking for a place to spend the night.

SOON I WAS in front of the public school of Mudang, one of the remote villages Pascal and I had hoped to visit, drying things out on the wall of a stone fence. A crowd of dirty, barefoot children gathered around me. The man in the sports jacket was the schoolteacher. He had received his education in Kunming. In the beginning he was reserved and distrustful of me, but after a few hours he became much friendlier. Next another man, the village chief, showed up. His legs were wrapped in heavy jute to protect against snake bites, and he carried a Burmese shotgun, the first breech-loading gun I had seen in private ownership here in South China; the others had all been simple muzzle-loaders. He spoke good Chinese, having spent time in Dali, Kunming, and other parts of China. He too was at first distrustful but soon warmed up considerably. Then other villagers came to see me, including the old lady whom I had frightened so badly. Some of them brought me fruit to eat. Inside the school the children recited lessons together in Chinese, and I noticed there was a basketball hoop in the corner of the school yard.

After school was out, the teacher, who gave me his Chinese name, Song Li, took me to his house for dinner. He lived in two tiny shacks. In one his wife was busy making cornbread, similar to what the Tibetans made, and stew from squash. More villagers came by to see me and some brought gifts of food. One man reached into a sack, then pulled out and handed me a scrawny, squawking chicken with its feet tied. The old lady I had scared brought me a small basket of roasted and pounded corn, and several other women brought apples and small peaches. A young villager came by with a baby monkey in a bag. He had shot the mother with a poison dart from his crossbow, which was now slung across his back. He tied a light cord around the neck of the little creature and let it out. Each of the villagers took turns grabbing the frightened animal by its head, putting their faces very close to it, and talking to it in authoritative and condescending voices. I asked if they were going to eat it. "No," the young teacher explained. "Not today. I still have the mother to eat. Maybe we will eat it the day after tomorrow."

The chief spent several hours talking to me. He told me there were telephones as far as the main fork of the Irrawaddy, that Chinese money was used everywhere in the Drung valley, and that many of the adults and most of the children could speak, read, and write Chinese. Most of the men had been to Yunnan, ridden on buses, and seen movies. Many of the households had a radio or tape player, and Chinese pop music, especially that from Taiwan, was popular. Most of the men had flashlights, wristwatches, and rifles.

I thought about Pascal's dream of meeting a people untouched by the outside world, and the collection of watches, needles, and plastic jewelry he had carried as gifts. He had spent five years researching for this expedition and the last two saving money, planning, and preparing. Pascal probably knew more about the Drung people and this valley than any other Westerner alive, but the only information available besides a short article written by a Chinese man was over a century old.

Early in the 1980s, for a variety of political reasons, China began a massive campaign to improve the living standards of minority people in the remote areas. Food, clothing, and Chinese education were the main thrust of this effort, and with these, the people were inevitably permeated with Chinese culture. Even with its relative isolation from China six months out of the year, the Drung valley had not escaped this effort and had been thoroughly "Chinafied," at least in its outward appearance. Except for a few minor details in the homes and a few articles of clothing and jewelry, the Drung people and their dwelling places were almost identical to those in other parts of China and South Tibet. The scenery was spectacular, but it is spectacular everywhere here.

Maybe in a way it is better that Pascal never arrived here, I thought as I ate cornbread and drank tea in the schoolteacher's house. Maybe for him it is better that his dream of coming to the Drung valley remains a dream.

LATER IN THE evening the schoolteacher, several other villagers, and I sat cross-legged on the floor in the smaller of the teacher's two little houses and drank jiu. This was serious business! A cup was filled to the brim and passed clockwise around the group until it was empty. Then it was refilled from a huge plastic jug and sent around again. I had difficulty explaining to the others that I didn't drink, so I sat and feigned a gulp each time it was my turn. Eventually we went back into the other house and ate more food, and then it was time for bed. I slept in the smaller of the two houses in the teacher's bed. He slept on the floor with two other men, and the wife and children slept in the other house, the one with the fireplace. It was bitter cold again, but my sleeping bag was almost dry, so I was reasonably warm.

The next morning nearly the whole village arrived to see me off. Many of them had infected wounds and bites they wanted me to treat, so I spent a few hours lancing abscesses, disinfecting wounds, and adjusting spines. The old lady I had frightened so badly had a two-day-old third-degree burn on her arm. It needed professional attention, but of course that wasn't available, so I cleaned it up the best I could and bandaged it, which she said gave her relief from the pain. I looked at the tattoos around her mouth and cheeks, fading now with age. In years gone by these tattoos had been administered to make the Drung women ugly so they would be passed over by Tibetans who came down the old slave trails and stole women for concubines. She wore the traditional handwoven jute garment, which was also unique to the Drung people. It, too, was sun-bleached and faded. Under this she had on Chinese trousers and a blue Chinese work jacket. None of the women under forty had the tattoos, and none of them wore the jute garment. I realized that what Pascal and I had hoped to see was already something of the past.

We ate my chicken for breakfast, with a lot of squash and bread. Then five villagers came with me to help carry my things and cross the river. They told me that the cable crossing over the Irrawaddy was extremely difficult.

We followed the Nabalo River for several hours until

finally we reached the Drung River, which is what this section of the Irrawaddy is called. Here there was a single cable suspended between two large trees. It was incredibly strenuous, even for a rock climber like myself, to haul across. The villagers scrambled over almost effortlessly, large globs of wet moss tied in front of their blocks of wood to lubricate the cable ahead. The old, frayed ropes we used to attach the wood blocks to the cable were made of jute, and I wondered if they ever broke, sending villagers to an icy plunge in the river below. Even without all of my gear, I had difficulty with the crossing. I realized I had pushed my body hard the last few days and needed to rest and eat well or things were going to start breaking down.

We passed many little distilleries built into the mountain along the trail. In some of these jiu was being made, but most of them were used to extract an oil from chips cut out of the trees that grew there. This strange extract had an odor similar to licorice, but I had no idea what it was used for, and I lacked the Chinese to ask.

When we reached the Drung village of Dingxindoa, I encountered my first policeman in the valley. He was of a different minority from the Drung but could speak Dulong and Chinese. When he questioned me I played Chinese-less, and eventually he left, saying good-bye in English. He seemed to be drunk. The village chief, a tiny Drung man about twenty-five named Shou Chuyuan, wanted to see my papers, but I pretended not to understand his request, and within an hour we had become good friends.

The teacher had taught me twenty Drung words, and I used one of these, *ka*, to buy a large chicken from a village woman. I immediately butchered and plucked it, then with Shou Chuyuan and his friends cooked a big meal. I found a tiny store, where I bought a case of cigarettes as a present for the villagers from Mudang who had come all this way with me and now had to travel all the way back. I shared a Power Bar with the villagers, and they loved it. But now I had only two left.

As in Mudang, I was told that I was the first foreigner to come this way, although once in a great while a Chinese would travel here for one reason or another. Most of the villagers came to see me. Again I slept in a bed. I guess someone else had to sleep on the floor somewhere, but I didn't know who or where.

THE NEXT MORNING I awoke early, kindled a fire, and cooked freeze-dried eggs, along with some instant rice. I was famished. This day I spent resting, eating, and taking photographs of the Drung people, many of whom brought by gifts of fruit and pounded corn, while I in turn gave them tea and plastic jewelry.

Now I had to make a decision. The next village had telephones, and if I continued on out of the Drung valley that way, there was no question I would be arrested; even worse, I would be arrested in Lucu district, where two years before Pascal and I had been caught twice. The only other option was to try to cross the high passes back to the Nu River, where I would again have to evade the authorities until I could cross the Nu Mountains into the Lancang basin. The last two days it had rained a lot, so I knew it was snowing higher up. Shou Chuyuan confirmed that the mountains, which only the strongest village men dared cross in the summer, were by now impassable for the winter. He said the road to Gongshan from Popo, the main road into the Drung valley, would also be closed in another week, or two weeks at the latest, and after this the only way to leave would be by following the Irrawaddy into Burma, where the borders were protected by Chinese and Burmese military. He added that some villagers, including himself, were hiking to Popo, and that I was welcome to come with them. They showed no fear of traveling with me, and I wondered what they thought of my unannounced intrusion into their world.

Tired from my travels, I knew that even going with them, which was the easy way, could mean six or seven hard days before I would reach the Chinese city of Gong-shan on the Nu River. At the same time, the possibility of being arrested again by the police or military frightened me. It was a hard decision, so I told him I would have to think about it.

Shou lived in a long, low house of rough-hewn logs that was divided into several rooms, the largest of which contained a heavy iron scale. This was the central trading point for both forks of the upper Irrawaddy, and it attracted a constant stream of tiny men with bamboo baskets strapped to their backs. Inside were things they had produced: corn liquor, large blocks of pitch wood, and the fragrant oil of the trees I had seen earlier. This oil was by far the most valuable item, fetching two hundred yuan for six pounds. All day long Shou collected, carefully weighed, and paid for these items, then stored them in the back of the large room.

BY THE MORNING of November 4 I had decided to travel downriver with Shou Chuyuan and his friends. I would try to stay free from the authorities as long as possible. I arose early and built a fire in what I guess could be described as the village cooking room. Every Drung village keeps a little building with a fireplace like this one, stocked with wood, salt, and oil, where single village men and stray travelers can cook their food. A tiny, pretty Drung girl of fifteen came up and helped me cook my breakfast, which I shared with her. Afterward she helped me string shiny plastic beads I had brought with me onto a strip of waxed nylon thread. She clapped her hands and giggled in delight when I placed the necklace over her head and she realized it was for her. Shou slept in until 9:00 A.M., then leisurely cooked his breakfast. I had some of his hot butter tea, similar to what Tibetans drink. The Drung also add eggs, oil, and vegetable bits to their tea, making it more soup than tea. Shou and I roasted some potatoes to eat on the road, and also took from a leather bag in the corner of the cooking room several handfuls of pounded corn each. This was a favorite snack.

We didn't leave until 10:30. In the days that followed, I would come to realize that the Drung people were never in a hurry about anything. Three other men came with us. They were in their early twenties, but were so tiny they looked like children. The loads they carried, though, would have put a crick in my back.

For the next three days we hiked slowly, rested often, and stopped in every village for tea, tsampa, and pounded corn. Shou and his friends consumed an incredible volume of alcohol. I was amazed that they showed little evidence of drunkenness. At each village there was someone who sold jiu, and they would all cheerfully chip in for the five yuan to refill each of their canteens, and mine, for the next hour or so of the journey. Each time we met another person traveling on the road we stopped, drank together, visited, smoked a few cigarettes, then unhurriedly started on our

way again. Almost every man we passed had a crossbow
and a small, monkey-skin quiver of poison darts. It seemed
that the favorite pastime, besides drinking jiu, was monkey
hunting. The crossbows, which the Drung made themselves,
were beautifully crafted. The bows were carved from solid
black hardwood and the stocks from wood of a lighter
color. String locks and triggers were made from solid ivory,
which I was told came up through Burma from India. No
metal was used in the construction.

THE FIRST NIGHT we stayed in the village of Langulen, and
here I saw the first phone lines, shiny new wires trailing
from the corner of the main building, a two-story Chinese-
style square cement structure. The village chief, a rough-
looking, stockily built Drung man in his mid- to late twenties dressed in a dirty green Chinese uniform, sprinted out
to meet us. He threw his arms around Shou in a rough bear
hug, then screamed hello to me in Chinese, shaking my
hand so violently I nearly lost my balance. Still gripping my
hand he grabbed Shou's jacket and dragged us both into the
building. *"Mei guanxi, mei guanxi"* ("Don't worry"), Shou
giggled, *"ta shi wo de pengyou"* ("he is my friend"). The
boisterous man poured us tea, spilling more on the floor
than into the cups, then went right for the phone, while I
hurried outside to use the bathroom. For two hours he
twisted the crank on the old-fashioned telephone and
screamed into the receiver, but all he got in reply was loud
static. We cooked dinner outside over an open fire pit, then
I retired early, to a bed I was shown to on the first floor,
while the rest of my traveling companions clumped up the
stairs to gamble and drink and party the entire night. Chinese music blared from the tape player, and occasionally

someone threw something heavy against the wall. Still, I was exhausted and slept. About 3:00 in the morning I was rattled awake by a loud crash and the sound of breaking glass, followed by a bloodcurdling scream. It was Shou's friend putting his fist through a window. The next morning it took me eighteen butterfly bandages to close the worst of the lacerations on his arm, after which I had a friend for life. He said his name was Nu Mall Gum, and that he would come with us—I'm not sure why. Perhaps he just had nothing better to do. He carried more than half my stuff on his back though, so I was happy to have him along.

Again it was late morning when we packed and started hiking. We followed the trail as it wound lazily through the village, past the single large house we had slept in, past the tiny elfinlike thatch-roof dwellings, and finally past the telephone pole near the edge of town where I had popped the wires off the insulators, then twisted them together with my folding pliers the night before on my trip to the toilet. (Pascal would have been proud.)

The entire day Mall Gum talked to me or, more accurately, shouted nonstop. His voice was incredibly hoarse, and it sounded as though he was severely angry about something. I knew the type: if you were his friend, he would die for you; if you were his enemy, he would just as soon kill you; and there was nothing in between. Luckily, I ended up being his friend, and during the next few days he treated me with incredible kindness.

When we came to the second village, all the villagers crowded around and I wasn't able to get away and "fix" the lines before the chief made a call somewhere concerning me. I figured I still had several days before anyone was likely to get around to doing anything about me.

TEN

The Dream of Flight

THE THIRD EVENING we reached the village of Kongmo. There were no cement buildings, but a large screen had been set up between poles and I was told that it was "movie night." Nearly every man in the village was drunk or semidrunk, including the village chief. I wondered if the Drung had always drunk this much, or if the Chinese had brought this vice to them. One inebriated man proudly took me into a small storehouse in which there were many shotguns and submachine guns. This village had a militia, just as in Ridong. I was given a bed in a house but told I would have to pay six yuan for it.

I had just started to lay out my things when the police arrived, two young Chinese men dressed in immaculately clean uniforms. Mall Gum came in with them and told me they were the police (which was obvious). I ignored them and continued to lay out my things. One of the young officers stepped forward and grabbed me, and the other slapped a pair of handcuffs on my wrists. His action was so unexpected I jumped up in surprise. They barked at me to sit down and demanded my passport. When I gave them a photocopy, they dug through my things until they turned up the original. Mall Gum became furious and started screaming at the policemen, but one of them shoved him outside and locked the door. Never before had I seen the

Chinese police act this aggressively on a first encounter. I wondered if they knew of my previous attempts to get here, or if they thought I was doing something I shouldn't. They searched my things, confiscating my ice ax, knives, maps, and passport. I managed to kick my journal under the bed and, surprisingly, they either showed no interest in or didn't notice my camera and film. After the search they unlocked the handcuffs and let me go to dinner, telling me to be careful of my money, that the villagers would steal it.

I ate with Shou Chuyuan and my other four traveling companions, cooking our dinner in a separate room from that of the village chief and policemen. The young Drung men were extremely upset by the situation and had a hard time eating the rice and fried potatoes we had prepared. Actually they were far more upset about things than I was, since I had known all along this was probably coming and was prepared for it. We ate quietly and visited. Shou told me they had decided to continue on with me to Popo, I think to make sure the policemen treated me right.

Over a hundred people showed up from the surrounding villages for the movie. A small electric generator was carried a hundred yards out of the village and started up. They showed three Chinese movies, which were silent, as the ancient projector was not capable of playing the sound. The village chief, still highly intoxicated, kept up a constant narrative in Dulong, and it must have been terribly funny because the crowd of villagers rolled on the ground in laughter. Only one other time in my life, while watching the *Rocky Horror Picture Show* with a theater full of Mormon rebels in Rexburg, Idaho, had I seen an audience get as big of a kick out of a movie as this crowd. I went to bed early so I could get up and hide my film while cooking breakfast.

One of the policemen put his bed close to mine and retired at the same time I did. I fell soundly asleep in minutes, in spite of the din the movie watchers were making.

AT 5:00 THE next morning I awoke, crept outside without waking the two officers, and built a fire in the community cooking shack. I made a large breakfast from my freeze-dried food, then put five rolls of exposed film into a half-full package of freeze-dried beef Stroganoff. I put in extra rice for padding, then resealed the package with glue from my air mattress repair kit. When the police got up several hours later, the villagers brought us chicken, potatoes, and squash and I ate again. Popo was still more than eighteen miles away, a two-day trip, but the policemen had left Popo early the morning before, and they told me that they wanted to make the return trip in one day too. I wouldn't agree to this, and neither would my five Drung friends, but the policemen told us bluntly we were going to do it anyway.

It rained all day and the hike was grueling. Two of the small Drung men took many things out of my pack and carried them for me. I was grateful for their help. The policemen carried very light day packs, but they didn't offer to help. The tension between the Drung men and the police was palpable. That morning my young friends had dug through the policemen's things while they slept and returned my ice ax, machete, and knives, and this made the officers furious when they found out. Having recovered from the initial shock of being caught, I had stubbornly refused to give them back.

As we hiked, we came to a place where a long, thin ribbon of water cascaded down from the gray, pockmarked limestone cliffs and formed a deep, still pool beside the path. Shou sang out, *"Xiuxi"* ("Rest break"), but the policemen angrily shouted back *"Mei xiuxi!"* ("Not a rest break!"). The Drung men ignored them and all plopped down on the ground anyway, motioning for me to join them—which I did. The policemen, furious at again having their authority contradicted, marched back, angrily grabbed my pack, hoisted me to my feet, and marched me on. Mall Gum screamed what sounded like profanity after the police. It made me mad too, and I felt like a captured animal. Ten minutes later, when we again came to a small stream and the police themselves announced that this was the rest stop, I shouted angrily, *"Mei xiuxi!"* and marched on past them down the trail. They followed, looking surprised and slightly confused. The two policemen then hiked right with me, one in front and one in back, so closely I felt oppressed.

By 1:00 in the afternoon we were only halfway to Popo, and all of us were tired, so we stopped for a cold lunch near the confluence of a small stream close to the Irrawaddy. The policemen had their own high-energy bars much like mine, and they shared one with me, so I shared my Power Bar, dried yak meat, and corn tsampa with them. Eventually the four Drung men caught up with us and we started out again. We were much too tired after lunch to continue playing mind games, and somehow sharing our food had relieved some of the macho animosity between us. They let me hike in front and set the pace, and whenever we came to a good rest spot, we rested without further discussion.

We passed many villagers on the trail who stopped and stared in unconcealed amazement. If they spoke Chinese, they inevitably commented, "So you're that foreigner who hiked down from Tibet!" Some of them gave me presents of food and, much to the delight of Mall Gum and Shou, sweet jiu (corn wine) and jiu (whiskey). One Drung man, dressed in a mud-speckled blue uniform and speaking good Chinese, beseeched me to take a photograph of him standing near the trail. *"Taiyang bu hao"* ("The sun is not good"), I said as an excuse, meaning the light for photography and pointing at the thick roof of clouds billowing over us. I didn't want to draw the policemen's attention to my camera. The man suddenly marched forward and stood in front of me, staring up into my face. His lips, flushed from alcohol, quivered slightly. *"Taiyang hao, taiyang hen hao"* ("The sun *is* good, the sun is *very* good"), he said, as if in rebuttal. And then, *"Taiyang shi shen!"* ("The sun is God!") I had forgotten that long ago, somewhere on our first attempt to reach the Drung valley, Pascal had said that the Drung worshiped the sun. I realized that I had been told this before, even since entering the Drung valley this trip, but my poor command of the Chinese language, coupled with the thick Drung accent, had kept me from understanding it till then. *"Taiyang hen hao"* ("The sun is very good"), I agreed in apology, then smiled and said to myself in English, "The sun is God."

The farther down we went, the more Chinese-style cement houses we encountered. The bridges changed from one-strand cable *"whee*-let's-slide" affairs, to two-strand cable bridges having crooked boards wired dubiously beneath for walking on, to proper steel-and-wood suspension bridges. We passed a small hydroelectric plant late in the afternoon, and from there on down all the villages had electricity.

In the evening we reached Popo, the village from which

we would cross into the Nu River basin. I wasn't allowed to go into the town at first but was taken to a group of large wooden houses, which turned out to be the police station. Immediately Shou Chuyuan and Nu Mall Gum fell into a bitter argument with the captain of the facility over the way I had been treated. They said that handcuffing me and then making me hike so far was terrible. I could only get bits and pieces of the discussion, but I understood Shou as he shouted again and again, "This is the Dulong River, not China! We own this river, not China! We are Dulong people, not Chinese!" These were pretty strong words coming from a man who was appointed by the Chinese government as a public official for the upper Drung River. Mall Gum got out of control. He screamed (of course, he always screamed) at the policemen, showing them the cut I had fixed on his hand. I was actually afraid he was going to strike someone, but he somehow managed to refrain. Eventually all four of the Drung men stormed off, shouting belligerently over their shoulders at the policemen. When they were gone, the police cracked up laughing.

One of the policemen who had escorted me kindly gave me his large, clean room, which had a television and a Chinese copy of a Nintendo video game. In all I counted fifteen policemen. Macho and arrogant, they showed open contempt to the villagers, although they treated me with undeserved kindness. We ate a delicious meal of Chinese food as good as I would have found in a fine restaurant in Chengdu, then watched the news on TV. It was obvious these weren't average policemen or military, but something special, some elite group, and as such they were given superior living conditions. They refused, however, to answer any of my questions concerning them or the surrounding area. The average age of the men was twenty-five, a little older than the soldiers at Ridong. Some of them were married and had their wives there with them. The men were energetic and rambunctious, and that first night I twice got into spontaneous wrestling matches. They were impressed with my hike down from Tibet and gave me many compliments about it, then asked many questions. We watched TV for several hours before going to bed.

THE NEXT MORNING after breakfast the police chief came to my room and told me it was imperative that I cross the mountains within the next week, as the passes would soon be closed for the winter. He said that last year four men traveling in the other direction had died because there was too much snow. The next day three men were planning to leave for Yunnan, and if he could get through on the telephone before then, he would send me with them. He also told me I wasn't allowed to leave the complex. After he went to his room, I took a basket of clothes as if I was doing laundry and hiked down to the stream a few hundred yards below the police complex. No one paid any attention to my leaving. I hid the clothes under the thick duff of the forest floor, then spent a few hours photographing the surrounding area. Later in the evening I hid the camera and went into the village of Popo.

Because Popo is the first Drung village on the trail from Gongshan, it's the focus of the Drung valley, with a bank, a post office, and at least twenty little shanty stores, most of which are owned and operated by Chinese, not Drung, people. I walked around the streets for half an hour, greedily buying and consuming candy, canned fruit, and soda pop. While walking along a little side street, I heard a low whistle and looked up to see Shou Chuyuan motioning to me from the doorway of a small house. He held his fingers to his lips in the universal signal to be quiet, looked cautiously around, then frantically waved again for me to come in. At least ten people were crowded into the tiny room, including Mall Gum and the three men who had accompanied me from the upper Drung valley. An old man and his wife were cooking food in the fire pit, and Shou Chuyuan told me they were friends of his parents' as they brought me food and tea. The room was dark with smoke because there was no chimney hole in the roof, but when my eyes adjusted, I noticed a man about my age dressed in a clean yellow shirt with a colorful cotton sheet wrapped around his lower body. His feet were in sandals.

"This is our Drung brother from Burma," Shou Chuyuan told me. His voice lowered. "He's like you. He's not really supposed to be here!"

"Do many people come here from Burma?" I asked, fascinated by this opportunity to meet a fellow outlaw.

"No, only a few. The way is difficult. They must follow tiny trails through the mountains at night. There is a very good road along the Drung River, but for the last few years the Chinese military have guarded that way."

I wanted to question this man further about why he had come here. Had he come for trade, or was he just visiting? He spoke no Chinese, however, and seemed uncomfortable with my showing such an interest in him.

Shou Chuyuan then introduced me to a hunter passing through the town, who sold me a beautiful crossbow and a monkey-skin quiver filled with bamboo tubes that contained poison darts. These I smuggled back to my room and hid within my pack. The rest of the day I washed and mended clothes and ate a lot of food. In the evening, when I went out to get my things off the line, I was surprised to find Shou Chuyuan and Nu Mall Gum playing Chinese checkers with several of the policemen. They grinned sheepishly at me, and I decided then I really didn't understand the relationship between these two authorities. Later, when Shou Chuyuan came to say good-bye, I gave him one of Pascal's watches and promised to send the pictures I had taken during our travels together. He told me not to let the policemen make me hike too hard over the mountains, that it was a three-day trip.

That night the police chief brought back my passport and maps. I didn't know why he gave them back to me, and I seriously considered leaving early the next morning and crossing the mountains into Burma. I didn't need to—things would be fine in a few days—but I still had a yearning for more adventure. By leaving at 1:00 or 2:00 A.M., I could reach the top of the mountain passes by early morning, and it would be much too late for them to catch up to me before I could descend into the rain forest on the Burma side. However, I had no idea what would happen to me in Burma, where real dangers might well exist, and I decided not to take the risk. I knew China was safe.

I LEFT WITH three of the young policemen, who arrogantly told me we would reach Gongshan on the Nu River in two days. I got out the map and measured the distance, about forty-five miles. The pass was twelve thousand feet, and I said that they could hike it in two days if they wanted, but my pack was heavy and I was going to take it easy. I sat down and refused to budge. I wasn't about to let them dominate me as they had a few days earlier; it was obvious that if I didn't cooperate their only options were to shoot me or carry me, both of which seemed unlikely. We argued for a while and finally they said if I would hike with them at their rate, they would take turns carrying my pack equal shares of the time. I agreed, on the additional condition that they allow me to take photographs during the trip.

After the sun came up, we began to pass hundreds of caravans carrying supplies into the Drung valley. It rained until we reached the tree line, then it snowed. There was soon a good foot of new snow, but the hundreds of animals kept the trail packed down. Some of the caravans had as many as sixty mules, and most of the packers were Tibetan woodsmen, although the Chinese police insisted they were all Drung. I shook my head in amazement as I realized these men couldn't tell the difference. Many Drung people were hiking back from Gongshan with ponderous loads of food, cooking pots, clothes, and other supplies strapped to their backs. "Nagum," I said in greeting whenever we passed one of the men. "Nagum," they would reply, faces beaming at being addressed in their own language. The policemen were surprised. They each had been in the Drung area for over two years and yet had not bothered to learn to say hello, good-bye, thank you, or anything else in Dulong.

We hiked hard, stopping only three times in twelve hours. The police kept their promise, though, and we took turns, one hour each, carrying my heavy pack. They carried only tiny day packs. One officer had congenitally dislocating kneecaps and his knees gave him trouble along the way, so I adjusted him several times, on each of our breaks and again that evening. We stopped for the night where a huge leaning boulder provided shelter from the rain. Nine men of the Lisu minority traveling back to the Drung River with their horse caravan had already built a fire and made a deep bed of bamboo. They showed visible anxiety when the police started taking over, but squashed together to make room and give us the best part of the bed. Then they put water on to boil, built up the fire, and served us tea. I felt it was wrong to sleep where the policemen put me, so instead I set up my shelter under a tree several hundred yards up the trail. We had another big "discussion" about this, but it would have come to a fistfight before I would have taken a Lisu's hard-earned bed. Eventually the policemen backed off and let me set up my camp.

I crawled into my damp sleeping bag and listened to the pick, pick, pick of raindrops striking the plastic above my head. Tomorrow I would be in the Lucu district. This realization brought a sudden burst of adrenaline. I was much more frightened of going back than I had dared admit. "But how long will it be?" I said soothingly to myself. "A few days? A week? Maybe two at the most?" Eventually the police would release me, and the worst thing they could do was kick me out of China—which I was leaving anyway. Using a sort of mental gymnastics I had learned as a child, I projected my thoughts forward in time, skipping past the imminent trouble of the near future to when these things would be nothing more than a good story. Christmas in Idaho with my family—everyone would be amazed by my pictures (providing I made it out with them). Shortly after that I would go back to school in California, back to the mundane world of schedules and appointments, of honking horns, congested traffic, pollution, and faces lined with stress. I took a deep breath, surprised at the poignant feelings of nostalgia that came prematurely for the simple life I was now leading. My heart began to beat faster as again I thought of leaving. For all their special training, these Chinese men were still city people, and I would have little trouble evading them in the high, desolate mountains. My mind raced. If I followed a semirandom route through this vast country and stayed in villages no more than a day or two at a time, how could the authorities ever track me down? I now knew from experience that the people along the way would feed me and give me the things I needed—freely, as well as in return for the healing I carried in my hands. There was a rushing deep within my stomach as I thought of the black bird I'd dreamed about. What if I became that bird? I could fly so far and so high nothing could touch me. In those high, ancient ranges, I could soar above and be free of the rules and drudgery that lashed out at me like the sting of birdshot, leaden legacies of a material world. I imagined getting down on my hands and knees on the sacred Do-Kar-La Pass, pressing my face to the earth like the pilgrims had to catch a glimpse of the hidden magic, the deep pulsing spiritual forces that coursed down from the mountaintops through the rivers and into the blood of this now-broken people.

For the last few months, as had been the case many times before in my life, I had walked increasingly closer to the fringes of society, tearing loose from invisible bands—expectations I felt the world had placed on me and ones I had placed on myself. Interrupting school and coming back to China to travel illegally with Pascal had started the process again. Leaving him and returning alone had brought me closer yet, and finally, somewhere in the freezing, wind-swept mountain passes between the Nu and Irrawaddy, a door to the most hidden part of my soul had cracked open, revealing what had brought me back to Tibet and to the edge of the world where I now stood. I had come here to find myself, and I had found that I was still my father's son. And I had come here to make a choice, between the hectic modern world I had left and the excitement of a world I had dreamed of. The line between enlightenment and insanity is a fine one. If I continued on and stepped off this edge, there was no question I would rise, pack my things, and disappear into the stormy night. *And then what would I become?*

It was something I would never know. I closed my eyes and I felt a great welling-up of joy, not because of the choice I had made to reject the fantasy—to go back and continue the life I had left—but because it *was* a choice.

ELEVEN

The Long Way Home

AS WE APPROACHED the town of Gongshan, I began to feel anxious. Would they figure out that I had been caught in Tibet before? Worse, and far more likely, would they call up Lucu and find out about our attempts two years ago? Would they find my film—or decide to keep my journal?

Upon arrival the three Chinese men immediately took me to the Gongshan police station, where I was hustled up to the fourth floor and taken into a nice office. A large couch near the door looked like a great place to hide things, so I immediately put my pack on it and sat down, acting much more exhausted than I felt. Moments later, two policemen entered, one about fifty and the other in his midthirties. Both were of the Lisu minority, their thick Chinese nearly impossible for me to understand. They questioned me about why I had come here, and I told them I was trying to get to Kunming from Tibet but had found the way to be very difficult and long. We almost couldn't communicate at all, and eventually they gave up trying and decided to search my things instead. I felt confident by this time because I thought they had probably never searched a foreigner before. I had also been searched several times by now and had some idea of what to expect and what I wanted found and not found. These men, however, were excruciatingly thorough. They found my money, which I had hidden in wool socks; my prayer flags (in another pair of socks); and several rolls of decoy film in the pocket of my bib overalls. The highlight of the search came when the older man found the can of Mace I carried for dogs. Not knowing what it was and refusing to heed my urgent plea to do otherwise, he sprayed a long stream into the air near his face so he could see what it smelled like. I was able to take advantage of the distraction that followed to hide my maps, journal, and unexposed film under the cushions of the couch. The worst part of the search was when they told me they were keeping my crossbow, monkey-skin quiver, machete, and prayer flags. They opened several packages of food, but luckily not the one with my exposed film inside. I shared my last Power Bar with them, but the older man was reluctant to try it at first, showing a great deal more prudence in general after his experience with the Mace canister. After the search the two policemen gave me back my passport, toothbrush, toothpaste, and money and told me to find a hotel and meet them back at the station the next day. When they weren't looking, I retrieved the items hidden in the couch. I walked out of the station feeling dazed, but also hopeful that I was going to get away without too much more trouble.

Gongshan was big and fairly modern, with several movie theaters, five or six hotels, and many restaurants. Most of the people were Lisu, although there were a few Drung and Tibetans, and of course the larger stores and important government positions were owned and filled by Han Chinese. As I walked around town, people approached me and shyly asked if I was the American who had crossed the mountains and entered the Drung River valley from Tibet. They said no one had ever done that before. I found a nice restaurant and ordered several plates of food.

"THAT MUST BE him!" I looked up in surprise. It was the first English sentence I had heard in nearly a month. Standing in the doorway of the restaurant were six Chinese people, but from their pile jackets and tailored jeans, I could tell they were foreigners like myself. The man who had spoken—he looked to be about forty-five—bounded over to my table with terrific energy and shook my hand.

"Hi. I'm Kinnie Lee from Taiwan. We heard about your journey from Tibet to the Drung valley. Will you join us for dinner?"

A manager in an American insurance company, Kinnie told me his great love was photography, and that it was his dream to preserve on film a record of all the minorities before they disappeared forever in the homogenization of modern China. His group had come to see the Drung valley.

"There are twenty-five minorities in Yunnan alone," Kinnie told me passionately as we ate. "You would not believe how much they have changed and how much has been lost in just five years! You saw the Drung people. Not much left, is there? A few of the old women have the tattoos. Some of them wear a piece or two of the traditional cloth, and they use the crossbows, but I tell you, even in a few years, all of this will be gone. They are building a road into the Drung valley. You probably saw the start of the construction. In five years when this road is completed, Dulong will completely disappear. But they will still exist in my pictures, and people will be able to open my books and see what the Drung were, and the Naxi and the Yi, and the Lisu." Kinnie was the second Taiwanese man to be allowed into the Irrawaddy basin, and he told me I was the first Westerner to reach the upper Drung valley, as far as anyone knew, and maybe the only Westerner still alive to have seen the Drung River and the Drung people.

THE NEXT MORNING I ate breakfast with my new friends. When they were ready to leave, I said good-bye and went to the police station. The two policemen who had searched me before said there was no one available to speak English for me. They paced around the room, picking up things and setting them down. I started getting nervous. Suddenly it hit me that they were simply at a loss for what to do. I asked them if I could bring one of the Taiwanese people up to talk to them, and they said there weren't any Taiwanese people here. I realized that the policemen were unaware that Kinnie and his group had come through. I couldn't believe it! I sprinted through the room, downstairs, and back across town to the hotel, thinking, Oh please, God, let them still be here!

"I'm sorry, they've already left," I was told at the desk. I roared outside and down the street, realizing that the police might keep me here for several days, until they transported an English teacher up from Lucu. Or worse yet, what if they sent me to Lucu to be questioned? Right now they didn't know what they wanted to do. This was my chance, if only the Taiwanese were still here!

Suddenly, I spied a member of Kinnie's group beside the creek—a pretty anesthesiologist who spoke English well. "Mei," I yelled. "Mei! Where's Kinnie?"

"He's having trouble getting the bus arrangements

worked out. You know, a money thing. It will be a little while," she answered.

"Mei, can you come up and translate with the police for me for a few moments?"

"Sure, I would be glad to." I decided not to tell her my whole story because I didn't want to involve her in any lies. She put on her jacket and followed me to the police station.

At first the policemen chastised her for not checking in with them when she arrived in town. For them I think it was a way to save face because they hadn't known what was going on around them. She apologized, then spoke smoothly and confidently about me as they asked simple questions.

"Why did you come to the Drung valley?"

"To get from Tibet to China."

"Do you know this area is closed to foreigners?"

"I do now."

They spent a few minutes gravely explaining the importance of keeping the law and doing my part to maintain the public security, then fined me one hundred yuan (about twenty dollars) and said I could leave with Mei and Kinnie. Mei, however, wasn't through. She kindly petitioned them to give me back my things. At first they said no, but after a little discussion they returned my crossbow, my nonpoisonous arrows, and my prayer flags, keeping the beautiful monkey-skin quiver full of poison arrows and the long machete. I was so grateful I couldn't think of a way to thank her.

Mei and Kinnie couldn't get me on their bus, so I wasn't able to leave with them as I had been told to. So the following morning I rode the bus to Lucu. There was much construction on the road, so the 120-mile trip took fourteen hours. Each time we stopped, people would come up and ask if I was the American who had crossed the mountains to the Drung River from Tibet. Even the road workers knew the story. The closer we came to Lucu, the more apprehensive I became. I had hoped to slip through Lucu without any contact with the police because, even though I had the travel permit obtained from the Gongshan police, I was worried about what might happen to me if they recognized me from two years before. When the bus finally arrived, any hope of making an unobtrusive pass through vanished immediately. Two policemen were waiting for me at the door of the bus. They grabbed my things and tried to hustle me down to the station. I threw a fit, showed them my travel permit, and insisted on buying my bus ticket for the next morning. Again they tried to make me go to the police station, but again I refused, telling them I was hungry and tired, and that I had already been fined in Gongshan. One of the men finally left, then returned with a Chinese woman who turned out to be one of the local schoolteachers. I was greatly relieved it wasn't one of the men who had translated for us two years before. One of them had written to me and asked for money several times after I had returned to America, so maybe the authorities had found out about that and quit using him as a translator. The woman's English was about as good as my Chinese, so we could only speak to each other simply. Again the police said they wanted me to take my things down to the station, that they wanted to search them and me. My adrenaline began surging. What was this all about? How much did they know about my adventure in Tibet, or the incident two years ago when the little girl we'd given candy to got sick? I had to find these things out fast and get these men on the defensive, as Pascal always did.

One of the men grabbed my crossbow and announced that I wasn't allowed to have it. I snatched it back and told him I had just traveled fourteen hours, and before I was going to talk to them, I wanted to get a room near the bus station and something to eat. They said no, but I ignored them and marched to the hotel. To my relief they helped me get the room and I put my pack on the bed. They told me to bring my pack with me, that they needed to search it, but again I ignored them and angrily shooed them out of the room, locking the door behind me. They followed me to the nearby restaurant, where I ordered a big bowl of rice noodles and slowly started eating.

"O.K.," I told the schoolteacher after my second bowl of noodles. "Tell them that if they want to talk to me, they can talk to me here!" The police told him that since I was the first foreigner to come this way to Tibet, they wanted to know the purpose of my chosen route, go through my belongings, and basically find out what I was about. Good, I thought, it doesn't seem as though they know anything. They went on to say that the Popo police had phoned them and asked that I pay two hundred fifty yuan in addition to my fine for their guiding me through the mountains. They said the route was dangerous and that I could not have made it alive on my own. Feeling proud, perhaps too proud, of my accomplishment, I laughed in their faces. "I hiked down from Tibet, where for three days there was no road, no people, nothing! The passes I crossed were much higher than the ones from Gongshan!" The teacher continued translating for us despite the mounting tension.

I told them the policemen who had been with me were weaklings, that in the end I had to carry them across the mountains one by one. It was incredibly disgraceful, I said, and really slowed me down! I figured if they could make up a lie, I could make up a better one. I continued on, telling them I had had to work on one of the policemen's legs because his knees were bad. I said I was a doctor, and in America my fees were very high, but because I knew the Chinese police were not very important in the Communist society and therefore had little money, I had done this for free. Since they were now trying to steal money from me, I would consider charging the police department in full for the services rendered. "Let's see. A chiropractic adjustment costs thirty dollars, or a hundred fifty yuan. I gave the man six treatments, which would be nine hundred yuan, minus the two fifty you are charging me. This comes to six fifty the police department owes me."

The two young officers stared at me in disbelief and were completely at a loss for words. I looked at my watch. It was 12:30, and we had argued for over three hours about this fine. My bus left at 6:00 the next morning.

"Look," I said suddenly. "I'll make a deal with you. I'm tired, and sick of this whole thing. I have met some very honest and nice Chinese people, even policemen, but you here in this Lucu district are thieves and liars. But as I said, I am sick of the whole mess so I will pay the fine, only on the condition that you go to the police station and bring me a receipt, and afterward I can go to bed."

They talked a little between themselves, then told me they agreed. One of them started to get up, but I grabbed his arm and shook my finger menacingly at him. "And I want both your names written on the receipt!" I let him go. The two men offered to pay for my dinner, which I refused, then walked me back to the hotel, buying the schoolteacher and me each a can of orange juice. At the door of the hotel they nervously told me that if I didn't agree with the fine, I could appeal it at the central police station at Kunming. I told them I certainly would, that I didn't agree with it at all. Pascal's lessons had served me well.

I BOARDED THE morning bus on time and breathed a sigh of relief as we drove out of Lucu. I was finally free—or, well, almost.

A military policeman entered the bus and walked slowly to my seat, where he stopped and regarded me sternly. "Passport, please," he demanded in Chinese. I felt a deep sinking in my gut as I saw his shiny new plastic-encased patch, which said, in English, BORDER DUTY. I realized this was the same division of the military that had arrested us in Tibet and wondered with anxiety how thorough their network of communication was. The soldier told me to step down from the bus and bring my things. I left my bag on the bus, and he didn't tell me to retrieve it. I was escorted to a small office, where a burly man sitting behind the desk said, "You are the American who traveled to the Drung River from Tibet. You are under arrest for traveling in a closed military area."

No! I wanted to scream. *Enough is enough! Can't you just leave me alone?*

I dug through my belt pouch and produced the travel permit, along with the receipts from the fines. I felt that these would do no good, but I had to try. The policeman carefully read the document, copied down some of the information, then handed it back with my passport and told me I could go. I couldn't believe it. I went back to the bus and again took my seat. A policeman slowly raised the huge iron gate. Suddenly another policeman flew from the door of the building and sprinted to the bus. I knew it couldn't be that easy! The man marched down the aisle directly to my seat, stopped, and opened his hand to reveal a two-yuan bank note. "You dropped this" was all he said. I thanked him in a shaky voice and in a minute we were off.

WE REACHED SHAGUAN late in the afternoon, and I caught a minibus the fifteen miles to Dali, the little tourist town nestled in the mountains above a huge lake bearing the same name. Suddenly I was surrounded by Westerners. Pink Floyd and the Grateful Dead blared from little food joints, and pretty women of the Bai minority served pizza, beer, and hamburgers to backpack travelers clad from head to toe in colorful outfits purchased in little hippie boutiques along the streets. As I strolled through the town, policemen stopped me twice to examine my crossbow. Eventually I reached a place called the Number Two Guest House, where Pascal and I had stayed on our first trip. Bits and pieces of conversation floated to my ears. A British guy was talking to an Aussie about rugby. Two Canadian girls were having a lively argument with an Australian girl about the decision to hold the Olympics in Sydney and not China. Someone was bashing Clinton. Outside the Tibetan Freedom Restaurant, a long-haired Katmandu dude was blowing sweet-smelling puffs of grass into the air while he delivered what sounded like a discourse on Taoism and the spiritual evolution of the universe to three similarly stoned European women. I could have sworn the same man, or perhaps his twin, had been here two years ago.

It suddenly occurred to me how dirty I was compared to others around me. Big-nosed, pink-faced barbarians like myself, as well as the local Dali people, wore clean, new clothes, had neat hair, and smelled good. I felt everyone staring at me as I entered the hotel lobby. A young woman wordlessly passed me the foreign registration form, wrinkling her nose in disgust and avoiding my eyes. She gingerly picked up by the corner the one-hundred-yuan note I passed her, then set the change on the counter and not in my outstretched hand. I took a dorm bed for two yuan and, after dumping my pack in the room, went out to buy a pair of jeans and a shirt. Next I trimmed my beard and hair, then took an hour-and-a-half hot shower that was pure joy. I put on the clean clothes and headed to a restaurant. I had forgotten how good it felt to be clean and to have new clothes.

In the Tibetan Freedom Restaurant I sat down and ordered four dinners. There I met a French couple, Jerry and Maude. They had met Pascal here three weeks before on their way to Tibet, and now, by coincidence, were back again on their way out of China. When they learned who I was and that I had been successful, they were very excited. "Oh, you made it!" Maude said. "Pascal was hoping so much that you would!" They told me two other French photographers had tried to reach the Drung valley from Yunnan at the same time Sophi, Pascal, and I were trying, but they had been stopped by the authorities.

"So you were the first."

Later I took my clothes to be washed. Such an amazing thing, to be able to pay someone a few dollars to do what would take the better part of the day by hand. On the way back to my room I found a note from Pascal in the letter box:

Dear Wade,

Hey brother, did you get to the Drung valley? I'm sure you did, so I'm looking forward to having news from you. Please write me or call me in Paris as soon as possible. I'm going to Vietnam for about a month, from November 22 to December 27. I will stay in Hong Kong until November 21 and will give your friends there your bag with your slides and a letter from me. If you need anything in Dali, ask Tunuman, the boss of the Tibetan cafe. He's a good friend of mine and knows me well. Wade, I'd have enjoyed to have been there.

Your friend, Pascal

Pascal had once told me, "Sometimes you need to do what you can, and then you have to be happy with what you have done." It had been a good thing to say at the time. Coaches, teachers, and of course my parents had so many times in my life tried to soothe the ache of failure with similar words. Yet try as I might, I could not remember a single moment that I had felt peace and satisfaction when my best wasn't good enough. At the time I thought it was just another of Pascal's cons. I had expected him to taste sweetness where I would taste it, and bitterness too. But climbing over dangerous mountain passes and surviving in the jungle were not Pascal's forte. He did, however, have some rare qualities of his own that I had come to envy.

That night my journey ended, at least the one to the Valley of the Drung. The journey of self-discovery and mastery of the spirit would continue on, of course.

And Pascal? A year later, on a clear evening in mid-September 1994, Pascal Szapu, having conquered his own dragons, would stand triumphantly at the head of the Forbidden Valley and realize his dream of meeting the Drung people.

FOR MANY DAYS I hung out in Dali, eating good food, Christmas shopping, and writing. I took one day off and went for a long hike in the mountains with some other travelers. We swam in a deep pool beneath a waterfall, sunbathed, and visited for several hours on flat rocks heated by the sun. In the evenings people came to my room to be adjusted and I traded back massages with an Israeli woman who was traveling with her sister. One night I met a tall Greek man, a photographer like Pascal who had practically lived in China for five years, photographing the minorities. He told me he knew a Belgian woman who had visited the Drung valley several years ago, although he himself had never been there. When he described how she had traveled, I knew she couldn't possibly have gone by such a route without entering Burma first, and so she had probably not been there. It was then I realized that something had changed for me.

In the beginning I had though it so terribly important to be the first person to go to this place; that was my prime motivation for taking off half a year from school and using my life savings. Back then I would have been terribly upset had it turned out that some other Westerner had beat us there. It would have ruined the trip. I was now fairly sure I was the first, at least in modern times, but I didn't know for certain, and perhaps I never would. But if I found out I wasn't, it wouldn't make that much difference to me. In the days to come, I realized it would not be important that I had been to a place no other Westerner had been, although this had been the carrot Pascal had used to lure me on this second trip and the fire that had driven me to try again alone after we had failed. But now that I had done it, although it was a fine thing to tell about, the fact itself didn't really mean a lot. What was significant for me was that on this journey to the the Drung valley I had finally been somewhere *I* had never been before, somewhere I had desperately needed to go. At the same time, I revisited some places I hadn't allowed myself to go in a long time and, through it all, had finally come to understand something about myself, something that I would find the words to tell my father when I returned to America. I'd tell him that I knew he would've liked for me to have been a great athlete, and God only knows how hard I tried—from the time I was born he had instilled in me a burning drive—and that he wanted me to be a great hunter like himself. But, well, I never made it to the Olympics, never even came close. But I got to the Drung valley—and if not a gold medal, I'd brought back the gold of the setting sun, silhouetted by prayer flags in the Irrawaddy Mountains.

About the Author

WADE BRACKENBURY WAS born in Idaho and lives in Springville, Utah. He has traveled and climbed widely, worked as a mountain guide, taught wilderness survival courses, and worked as a chiropractor. Recently, he served as expedition doctor on a photographic mission up a tributary of the Congo River in Africa.